T0196386

——DARK——
SECRETS

DARK SECRETS

CHOOSING YOUR CHILD'S SPORTS COACH

SUZIANN REID

authorHOUSE®

AuthorHouse™ LLC
1663 Liberty Drive
Bloomington, IN 47403
www.authorhouse.com
Phone: 1-800-839-8640

www.SuziannReid.com

Published by AuthorHouse   07/26/2013

ISBN: 978-1-4817-5590-0 (sc)
ISBN: 978-1-4817-5591-7 (e)

Library of Congress Control Number: 2013909510

Any people depicted in stock imagery provided by Thinkstock are models, and such images are being used for illustrative purposes only.
Certain stock imagery © Thinkstock.

This book is printed on acid-free paper.

Contents

Dark Secrets

Drugs in Competitive Sports

A step by step guide for parents about how to find the right sports coach and to help their children become true legendary athletes.

Editor's Note

When Suziann Reid asked me to undertake the task of editing her manuscript it was a revelation to me. It was also a beam of light which highlighted the fact that not all people in sport are cheats. The media thrives on scandal and bad news and cheating sports stars have given them plenty of headlines. That tends to distort our idea of how prevalent drugs are in sport.

We have seen some huge scandals about drugs in sport, and it still continues. Even in the Olympics of 2012 there were people getting caught. How many escaped?

A US professional sports association carried out an anonymous survey of its Major League players, and 104 admitted having used illegal drugs of one form or another. 600 other Major League players were innocent. That's 1 in 7 cheats in that one professional sport. Is it a lot? It's certainly too many.

Suziann trained with and knows several athletes who became household names, first for sporting success, and then for very public falls from grace as their drug-assisted training regimes were exposed. Hence the title 'Dark Secrets'. Her background, principles and strong religious faith kept her clean when so many of her colleagues stumbled and fell. She has seen it from the inside and it is clear that most of the fallen athletes she knows blame their coaches. Well they would say that, wouldn't they—after all it's easy to blame the coach?

The point is that there are clusters of 'fallen' athletes around particular coaches. Most coaches are ethical and straight, but it is the few bad ones who cause the problem.

For young people just starting to get serious about their sport and adopt the rigorous training regimes and high commitment that success requires, shortcuts can be tempting, Some young sports people can be easily swayed when the coach says 'your competitors use human growth hormone. You have to match them or you are wasting your time—and mine'.

So, how do you keep your child on the right path to winning? Suziann Reid proved it can be done, and she gives you the benefit of her wisdom here, helping parents find the right coach (and avoid the wrong ones). To do this, she provides a basic picture of the coaching business, what motivates coaches, their ethics and even guidance on how to interview a coach. Then, there are a few gems from her on providing moral and other practical support for your budding champion.

If things go well for your young sports star and the opportunity to become a professional sports person is there, then Suziann's advice includes what to expect and how to plan the big transition.

Suziann is too modest to talk about her own achievements, so I'm going to tell you. It is important that you understand them—her considerable athletics record show what can be done without drugs and gives her the authority to talk about the issues. So, here are selected highlights of an outstanding athletics career:

- ❖ *United States Track and Field World Medalist*
- ❖ *University of Texas Hall of Honor Inductee*
- ❖ *2000, 2001 USA Indoor champion*
- ❖ *2001 Goodwill Games gold medalist (4x400)*
- ❖ *1999 World Champs silver medalist (4x400)*
- ❖ *3-time NCAA Outdoor 400 champion; 2-time NCAA Indoor 400 champion*
- ❖ *1996 US Junior champion; silver medalist at 1996 World Junior Championships*

You can find out more at the official <u>US Track & Field site</u>

James Marinero
Editor

Acknowledgements

I would like to thank God for blessing me with the natural gift of running, and allowing me to impact others in a positive way.

Thank you to my parents, Glenroy and Maria Reid, for nurturing and supporting me during my sports career. Without your love, guidance, and dedication, it wouldn't have been possible.

Thank you to Peter and Jacqueline Browne for your love, friendship, and support during my childhood years.

Thank you to Lawrence "Larry" Leahy, former Hyattsville Middle School Vice Principal that discovered my talent during a field day event.

Thank you to Coach Larry Colbert, my high school coach at Eleanor Roosevelt High School, and the founder of the Glenarden Track Club in Glenarden, MD. Thank you for teaching me discipline, courage, and true sportsmanship in sports.

Last but not least, thank you to my editor James Marinero for being so patient with me, and helping me to put together this great book. I couldn't have done it without you.

Introduction

I love sports and the excitement that it brings. As a young athlete in high school, I' always dreamed of becoming a legend in running. I admired and wanted to be like the greatest athletes of all time. My parents believed in my dream, and just like any good parents, they were right behind me to make it happen.

I was blessed to have their assistance and support as I followed my dreams to a professional level in sports. Along the way up the ladder in my professional career, I've discovered a few secrets. Some of these secrets can lead an athlete and their family to what it takes to become a champion in sports. Other secrets are darker, hidden secrets. They are pitfalls to avoid along the path to true success in sports.

Many parents dream of their child becoming the next Michael Jordon or Tiger Woods—a great sports icon for their time. What few parents realize ahead of time is that there are countless of dark, hidden secrets in the sports world that can cause heartbreak and pain to an athlete and his or her family. Without knowing these dark secrets, it is virtually impossible for an upcoming young athlete to avoid them.

Unfortunately, only a small percentage of the world's greatest upcoming athletes will avoid these dark secrets and instead follow a steady path that will lead to a sports career filled with fame and success that lasts for lifetime. I feel blessed to be one of those passionate few who pursued a career in running and was able to accomplish great lifetime achievements. I attribute this success to my parents' guidance, my faith in God, and others who helped me along this path.

Parents, without knowing certain pitfalls to avoid, might not take on the role they are meant to take as parents of young athletes. It would be like leaving a baby unattended in a crowded city. Anything could happen. As a parent wishing the ultimate best for your child's success, it's important that you know the hidden information about certain pros and the cons in sports, all the way from the little leagues to the professional levels.

Because of the various predators in our sport society who strategically plan and are patiently waiting to prey on innocent new and upcoming athletes, it is a dire necessity for parents to consistently monitor the safety of upcoming young athletes who dream of becoming Superstars.

More often than usual for other vocations or lifestyles, we see or read of top athletes in the news as they are being scrutinized or getting banned from their sport because of scandals. Countless top athletes are making terrible career mistakes every day, and their names are remembered as dishonest or scandalous to their sport. This causes severe damage to the athlete's career. Sadly, the athlete's families, teammates and fans, as well as the younger generation of athletes, get hurt in the process.

Nobody wants a bad name that carries the history of shame and disgrace. And nobody, when reaching for their dreams, believes that they will experience these pitfalls. However, they are widespread and common and therefore, very difficult to avoid, especially in the world of sports.

This book has been written to encourage you as parents in how to support and guide your upcoming superstar athletes as well as inform and warn you about the unseen dangerous pitfalls—the dark, hidden secrets in the sporting world today. They have power to shatter precious dreams and make it impossible to pursue a successful career as an athlete. It is meant to be a guide as you work with your child or teenager to "map out" the road he or she will take toward great achievements in the sports world.

There are a number of athletes who have risen to levels of fame and popularity, whose achievements will be long remembered by those who follow after them. Unfortunately, only a small percentage of the world's greatest athletes will take the time out to draw a map and reveal the hidden pitfalls and secrets in order to help other upcoming athletes to find their way to unlimited lifetime success in sports.

I believe it is my duty to teach and inform you as parents of upcoming superstar athletes what to look out for in the sports world and how to guide your children to be successful and responsible athletes.

My parents certainly did that for me. I hope that in some way this book will give you access to wisdom how to help your young champion reach the highest level in sports and be remembered as true legends.

The tips given and secrets revealed in this book are priceless and can be used to reach the greatest level of any sport.

I hope you will find guidance and inspiration as you read this book and use the instruction and tips I give you to guide and mentor your children as they follow their dreams and reach for the stars.

Part One

'I can do all things through Christ who strengthens me.'

Philippians 4:13—in the Holy Bible, New Kings James Version.

As a parent of a young athlete who is inspired to become a legendary athlete leading to an Olympic or a professional career, it is essential that you take the time to learn about the sports world that your child has begun to enter or will soon enter.

It is exciting for any parent to know that their child is skilful and talented at a sport, especially if the young athlete is focused and is striving to be the best. The early years of this development is critical for your young athlete and it starts with your guidance and support.

So many talented young athletes in sports are not receiving consistent, positive guidance from their parents. It is easy to find reasons for this; parenting is a huge job. You are often busy, sometimes absent due to work, or distracted by daya-to-day concerns. Yet your child needs

1

you. Young athletes cannot build themselves into legendary athletes without the help of their parents. They cannot teach themselves respect, trust, responsibility, and common sense. They need you to teach them first, and as they progress in their skill, other important sport figures will step in to help guide your young athlete's career.

There is no magic formula to ensure your child's success, but if you take the time from the start to share a bit of yourself, 'it will be like a seed that's planted. It will take root and eventually grow and blossom and bear the fruit that is desired.

I was blessed with parents who had experience in sports from a young age. Both my parents were active in sports at their primary schools in Jamaica. Like most parents, they continued in their sports education up to high school but neither of them pursued a professional athletic career. With that said, that does not mean parents should have an athletic background to create athletic superstars. You can do it, even if PE was your least favorite subject in school!

In this section, I'll define the essential steps needed for you to take to prepare your young athlete for the true sports world. Just like any system, to reach success, it is important for you to follow through each step to enable your child to reach unlimited success in his or her sports career.

Cultivation

> *'When God's children are blessed with talent in sports, they should use it wisely to bring Him the glory.'*
> —*Suziann Reid*

One essential step that you need to take in preparing your child for the true sports world is properly cultivating his or her body, mind and spirit. A child must understand the power of their body, mind and spirit and the synergistic roles they play in reaching maturity and success.

A good example is viewing your young athlete like a growing tree. Whatever you apply to the roots of a tree from the seed stage, it will show up in during the growth of the tree's life. With young athletes in sports, it is the same concept. Framing and cultivating the mind from the start will make a positive difference in their preparation for the future.

In order to effectively cultivate your child's mind in a powerful and positive way, you must live your life as an example. Children mimic what their parents do when least expected.

Suziann Reid

Cultivating the Body

> 'But those who wait on the Lord
> shall renew their strength; they shall
> mount up with wings like eagles,
> they shall run and not be weary,
> they shall walk and not faint.'
> —Isaiah 40:31

Eating healthy foods is one way my parents cultivated my mind at a young age. My parents would always tell me, "Your body is a temple. Value your body and it will value you."

My mother was big on preparing home-cooked meals for the family. She constantly made sure the entire family ate the right kinds of power foods to sustain us throughout the day. Our family rarely ate junk food, so at a young age I knew the importance of not putting anything unhealthy in my body.

Too often, parents make the mistake of rewarding their children by taking them to fast-food restaurants. As a result, young athletes cultivate a mindset of not valuing their bodies and eating whatever they want. This is taught—sometimes subconsciously—from an early age by the parents.

Nurturing the body with healthy foods takes discipline and, if taught early in a young athlete's life, it will become a part of their life forever. Teach your children to value their bodies by eating healthy foods yourself and by making it a priority to prepare healthy meals and snacks for them.

Basics of Body Growth

I know what you're thinking—what's body growth got to do with choosing a sports coach?

Actually, it's got a lot to do with it. I mentioned earlier that my parents took care to ensure that I was well nourished and that we rarely ate any junk food. That gave my body the best start in life, and meant that when I was on the sports field I could perform to the best of my physical ability, that I was less likely to get injured and that I could recover more quickly if I did suffer an injury. And I proved it—I didn't need drugs to succeed. That's the key.

In this chapter I'm going to tell you a little about how fast our bodies grow, basic nutrition and how to tell if your child is getting bad advice from a coach. Then, I'm going to tell you a little about the dangers of overtraining a young body.

Amazing!

'The blessing of the Lord makes one rich, and He adds no sorrow with it.—Proverbs 10:22 in the Holy Bible, New Kings James Version.

The human body is an amazing entity—it can store energy and the chemicals it needs, compensate for shortages at any time (with exceptions) and automatically keep its chemistry in balance automatically. When I came out of the starting blocks, the explosion of energy was instant and natural, accelerating my body to almost 25 mph in less than ten strides. That took dedication and training, but I couldn't have done it without proper nourishment.

Young bodies need energy to move around, and the brain uses 30% of the body's energy. Youngsters also need an excess of energy and nutrition to help them grow. The rate of growth is governed by Human Growth Hormone which is produced in the pituitary gland from the food we eat. We'll talk more about HGH later in the book, because it's a key chemical available as an illegal drug (for sports people)—and it gets abused.

How fast do Young People Grow?

The rate of growth differs between boys and girls. Girls usually stop growing 2-3 years after their first period. Boys—young men—don't stop growing until they are 25, but by the age of 22 growth has just about stopped. Here are some curves of body weight against age to give you the picture.

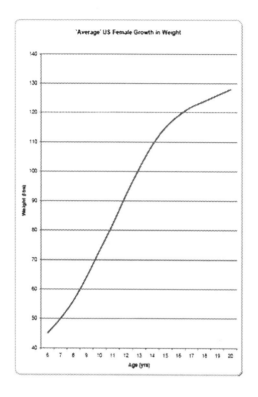

Where the slope is steepest is where youngsters have their 'growth spurt' and it's during this time that they will never seem to stop eating! This is where THG changes the hormonal balance, steepening and lengthening the growth curve so that the young body grows faster and for longer. Please note that these are <u>average</u> curves—don't use them to assess your son or daughter's growth progress.

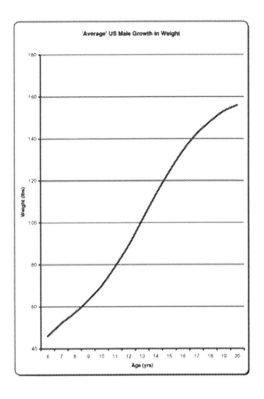

Notice that I've shown average weight against age and not height. Height curves vary from country to country, and here in the US we are not the tallest. It's the Dutch who take that honor! Height is important in many sports because longer limbs give greater leverage; but it doesn't apply in every sport. For example, great height is not an advantage for sprinters or weightlifters.

The importance of balanced nutrition cannot be overstated. Growing children have different nutritional needs to that of adults. Nutritional requirements depend also on activity levels and the particular sport.

A good coach will be able to provide specific advice, but the worst kind of coach may encourage the use of drugs to accelerate growth and grow muscle bulk. This could permanently damage the health of your adolescent athlete, besides resulting in a ban from competition (or other sanction).

Long term physical and mental damage might also result.

What is Good and Balanced Nutrition?

The body needs five basic food groups. The main food groups are: Fruit and vegetables, Carbohydrates ('carbs')/Starches—bread, potatoes, rice and pasta, Dairy (and dairy products), Proteins—meat, fish, egg and beans, Fats and Sugars. A balanced intake of all these food groups will provide a healthy nutrition balance, provided that the food is fresh and of good quality.

In the Appendix, I have included some basic nutritional advice.

Foods and drinks high in fat and/or sugar contain very few nutrients and are sometimes known as 'empty calories'. They should be eaten sparingly, even though they are an important energy source. This is junk food territory. The body stores excess fat and can convert it to

9

energy when required, but it's not efficient and it's not healthy.

One more point: being a vegetarian will not deliver success—and that applies in all sports.

Some essential chemicals known as vitamins cannot be stored and have to be replenished regularly—usually daily. That's why we have the phrase 'an apple a day keeps the doctor away'. For example, most fruit provides vitamin C, but there are 13 vitamins we need—and that requires a balanced diet.

Endurance sports require a different diet regime to 'burst sports', and there are sports which fall between these extremes. The best coaches will know what is best for their given sport and advise additional intake, depending on the particular sport. The worst coaches will look for shortcuts—illegal drugs.

Why Overtraining is Bad for Young Bodies

As I said earlier, this is directly related to body growth. During growth, the body is gaining on average a few pounds of weight every month. Nutritional intake is being used to keep it going—running, jumping and competing—and to actually add new cells. The body grows by cell division and that requires both fuel and building materials.

Here is a simple model:

Think about a new stone wall being built with cement holding the stones together. Now, when the cement is wet and soft, the wall is easily pushed out of shape. If it's not corrected then the cement will harden and the wall will be permanently out of shape.

For the growing body, think of protein as the stones (the bones, cartilage and other organs) with the connective tissue as the cement. There is one difference though—these stones are soft until maturity—it takes years to harden them.

Overtraining a growing body can deform joints and damage other tissue. Some damage could be permanent. Impact sports (and that includes running) and sports such as weightlifting are prime candidates. The younger the athlete, the greater the risk.

Fine, you heard the saying 'no pain, no gain'?

That's a great reason for finding the right coach. A good coach will provide a training plan which avoids overtraining, but just takes a young athlete through the pain barrier at appropriate intervals.

An unscrupulous coach will exceed the sensible training limits and may encourage the use of drugs for various purposes such as masking pain or putting on muscle bulk at an excessive and unnatural rate. Masking pain so that training or competition can continue may cause permanent damage to the body.

Cultivating the Mind

> 'Heaven has all the resources, and
> God has all the power. What more
> do we need to succeed?
> —Thomas Nelson, in God's Best
> for Your Success

Did you know that over 90% of the challenge competing in sports is mental? Without the proper mindset taught at a young age, it is impossible to become a great athlete.

One of the best ways my parents cultivated my mind from a young age was by having family meetings—every Saturday as long as I can remember. We used to have a set time for discussion and prayer. Everyone had the opportunity to express their thoughts about anything they wanted. My parents' goal was to make sure that the entire family was on the same page. By doing this, my brothers and I were taught how to control our minds to think and do things that were positive for us, for our family, and for the community.

So often, parents are too busy to take the time to train their children's mind. It's not easy because it takes effort. It takes a lot of time and patience, with yourself and with your child. But with proper training and nurturing of your child's mind, they will automatically think optimistically *and attract positive influences in their sports career.*

Besides using simple family meetings to cultivate a child's mind, parents can also reinforce positive ways of thinking by encouraging their child to live a disciplined lifestyle. Every day after school there was a list of chores I had to do in the house. I couldn't take any shortcuts. All chores had to be done right. My duties after school were easy and simple to do, but they instilled in my mind how to be self-disciplined and follow through with tasks.

Cultivating the Spirit

> *'It matters not how many times you fail—what matters is the successful attempt, which should be remembered, reinforced, and dwelt upon.'*
>
> —*Vince Lombardi*

The next step is the importance of cultivating your child's spirit. This is by far one of the most important because it touches the soul and heart—the conscience. You don't have to be religious to be spiritual. It is merely a form of awareness that goes beyond the things you can see and feel.

A child needs to understand the importance of knowing and growing their spirit. This can be taught by the parents if done consistently and correctly. Love is the primary component to nurturing your child's spirit. My parents respected my spirit by listening and communicating.

"Through the heart and the spirit a man speaks," my father would say.

"Feed your spirit the right things," my mother would often tell me.

My parents made sure the activities I took part in were uplifting and educational. I was not exposed to explicit programs on television but instead to positive ones. They also taught me the power of reading books that were nurturing and inspiring—well known Bible stories of triumph and many other classic children's novels.

There are many ways to nurture your child's spirit, and they all work together.

Giving your time and attention on a consistent basis is the best way to cultivate a young athlete's body, mind and spirit.

Competition

> *'And also if anyone competes in athletics, he is not crowned unless he competes according to the rules.'*
>> *—2 Timothy 2:5, The Holy Bible, New Kings James Version.*

Competition is the main factor in sports. Without competition, there wouldn't be sports. Competition exists in many aspects of life—from sports to careers, from relationships to education, you name it. Competition is everywhere and it is alive and well. It is important to teach your child from a young age how to face the "real world" of competition, especially in their sport.

When I was a child, I was extremely shy. I avoided confrontations and challenges in everything—but I loved sports. Most children tend to be shy until they gain enough confidence in themselves, then they snap out of it. In sports, one cannot be shy. To teach your young athlete how not to be shy might take time though, as well as patience and constructive input.

My parents knew that I had an amazing talent to run, so they nurtured it by helping me get over my shyness. Being timid is ok to an extent, but it was important for me to understand the importance of being assertive if I wanted to win my races.

Winning is about an athlete asserting superiority in an event—demonstrating it, publicly. I had to learn how to be aggressive rather than hesitant. This took time, and during the process I was probably a bit more withdrawn than my athletic peers.

I remember a specific time when my parents taught me about confronting competition. It was a race I'll never forget. I was a freshman in high school at the time and I made it through the qualifying round to enter the finals of my race. I was very excited and then all of a sudden I felt worried and sick to my stomach.

My reaction about facing the final competition of all the best athletes in the championships made me feel ill. Yet I knew I couldn't just back out of the race; I had to face my competitors the very next day. That night I couldn't sleep because I was so worried about what I would' encounter. I was a mess.

The next morning at breakfast, my father noticed that I was very quiet and wiping away tears at the table. When he asked what was causing the tears, my tears increased. Realizing that I was nervous, he told me something that made me feel so much more confident.

He said, "Suziann, believe in yourself and just do your best in the race. Everything will be alright. Just have fun with it."

When my father encouraged me at the table, I felt so much better. I felt lighter and more focused to run my race. That's what it takes to help your child to understand and approach their competition. Just saying those encouraging words when your young athlete is not feeling confident will immediately help in amazing ways. It will also help them understand that whether or not they are the fastest or whether or not they "win the gold" they are loved and supported. That will give them an inner strength and a confidence that cannot be shaken.

Never be harsh with your child during such times. Instead, use the time to teach your child how to mentally handle the pressure of competition. They will love you for this, and it will allow your child to be more comfortable to express their feelings about any anxiety and fears they have about the competition.

The beauty about competition in sports is that it teaches your child how to be a leader in their life. So continue to encourage your child every chance you get about how to be brave and face their competition. It will go a long way.

Respect

> '*Sheer ability is not enough to succeed in life, at least not for the long haul. Personal integrity is basic to long-term success.*
> —*Thomas Nelson, in God's Best for Your Success*

My parents use to always tell me, "Respect will carry you right through the world." I've proved this is to be true up to today. In sports, respect is central. Without respect, there would be disorder on every angle. It is essential for your child to understand the importance of having respect for themselves, for other athletes, and for their sport.

Today, a lot of athletes in sports take this important word very lightly. As a result, there is an evident lack of desire from some athletes to show respect towards sports and even their fellow competitors. They do themselves a disservice.

Respect for Self

Parents play a very important role in helping their child come to understand the essence of respect and it starts at home. For a child to have respect for others, they must first respect themselves. They must see the value in themselves. When they understand this, you'll see the results in their performances in many areas of their life.

It is not only their performance in sports that will improve, but also their academics and social life. All areas of their life will be in harmony if your child understands his or her self worth.

A key element in helping your child learn self respect is showing them unconditional love. Let them know clearly that your love and respect for them is not based on their performance. When they are assured in your love and support, regardless of how they perform, they will understand that their worth goes beyond their actions. This will speak volumes to their heart and increase their sense of self-worth and self-respect. It will enable them to experience both success and failure without fearing either one. They do not have to fear failure, because they have your love and support to fall back on, regardless of the outcome.

This love will help them to push their talents and skills beyond what they believe possible. When they realize this, they will be ever striving for greater achievement.

Respect for Others

> *'My grace is sufficient for you, for My strength is made perfect in weakness.'*
> *2 Corinthians 12:9—in the Holy Bible, New Kings James Version.*

When I was a young athlete, my parents used to encourage me to show respect to my competitors before and after my races. They thought this was very important because showing respect for the other athlete states that I'm a leader. I would do this by saying, simply saying "good run" to another athlete if I won, or congratulating my competitor if they won. That showed a lot of respect, and, since I practiced this principle from a young age, it enabled me to have sincere respect for others.

From a competitive perspective, it is stated simply as:

"Don't underestimate the competition."

There is more to it than that. Share with your child the concept that every competitor they race or play against is a unique individual, with their own dreams and visions for the future. When he or she sees others as just the same as them, it breeds respect.

Show respect and you gain respect.

Respect for the Sport

> *'If you want to win, play by God's rules.'*
> —*Thomas Nelson, in God's Best for your Success*

Another way I was taught to have respect was for my sport. In every sport there are rules and regulations that must be obeyed. If an athlete ignores or 'doesn't follow them, then the athlete will face consequences. Just like having rules in a home and the need to follow them, a young athlete must understand that it is essential to respect their sport.

As a parent, it is important to take the time to have open discussions with your child about the importance of respecting the rules of sports. Your young athlete must understand the big picture of having respect for the sport they love. My parents would often demonstrate the importance of this by conducting discussions about the consequences given to other athletes that broke the rules in their sport.

We would often discuss athletes that were broadcast on the news because of their behavior. During our discussions, we talked about athletes that were caught in fights with other components, skipping practice, being vulgar during interviews. We also discussed the consequences for cheaters that got caught using performance *enhancing drugs. All the athletes that did these things and more ended up in shame and disgrace. Usually, their sport careers collapsed and fans and spectators lost love and respect for them.*

It would be a major disappointment and a waste of time for an athlete to put so much time and work into their sport and then lose credibility for not respecting themselves, other athletes and their sport. Take the time to teach your young athlete the importance of respect. It is time well spent that will make a difference in their future success.

Integrity

> *'Better is a little with righteousness,*
> *than vast revenues without justice.*
> *—Proverbs 16:8*

One of the greatest lessons a parent can teach their young athlete is how to have integrity for themselves and their sport. Without the safeguard of integrity instilled in a child's mind from an early age, there is no telling what will happen later on in their life. This could be the making of a winner or a loser in sports and in everything else a child grows up to accomplish in his or her life.

When I was a young athlete, my parents played a very active role to make sure that my brothers and I operated with integrity. This was a very important family virtue.

I can remember several times getting scolded for not doing things honestly when I was a young child. My parents created a system to make sure we were in line and my brothers and I faced consequences if we were caught not completely following through with our studies in school, our daily chores around the house, and our dealing with friends and in the community. My parents wanted us to do things honestly and in the right way.

One day I was caught skipping school with some friends. My teacher noticed that my friends and I were absent from extra lessons class, so he decided to walk around the school building to see if he would find us. At the time, my friends and I were having fun playing in the school yard and didn't see the teacher slowly approaching us. Terrified that we had been seen, we took off running to avoid punishment.

The following day I was so scared to go back to school. When I arrived at class, the teacher told me that I could not come back unless I brought a parent to meet with him. I was so scared because I knew I was going to be in serious trouble with my parents.

When I got home, my father was preparing to go to work. He was very surprised to see me home and he knew right away that something was wrong. I then told him that my teacher wanted to talk to him about something I did that I shouldn't have.

My father and I went to the school and my teacher explained that he was very disappointed with me and my friends for skipping class and then running from him in the school yard. My father was angry with me because he trusted that I was going to all my classes. The most embarrassing part was getting scolded by the teacher in front of my father. From that day, I never again deceived myself and hurt my integrity by skipping school. That lesson taught to be honest and not cheat myself.

When there are no consequences for dishonesty and lack of integrity, a child will grow to assume that it's not a big deal, and will most likely develop bad habits in these regards.

My family was not wealthy, but my parents made sure that we had enough to make it through each day. "Putting hard work in everything you do will always pay off," our parents would tell us. We were also taught to believe that we could achieve anything we wanted in life if we diligently and honestly worked towards our goals. There are no shortcuts.

Spending time with your young athlete and training them about the power of integrity will inevitably prepare them for the journey to become great athletes. In addition, your child will be prepared when faced with pressuring influence to cheat themselves or others in their sport.

Adversity

> *"I've missed more than 9000 shots in my career. I've lost almost 300 games. 26 times, I've been trusted to take the game winning shot and missed. I've failed over and over and over again in my life. And that is why I succeed."*
>
> —Michael Jordan

When things go badly in sports, it is an adversity that must be perceived in the proper way to continue on the path to success. Professional athletes who have been in the sport for a long period of time usually are able to balance the failure with the many positive outcomes they have had and the experience that tells them, "Life goes on." Young athletes do not have a lifetime of experience that helps them know how to handle failures. To them, it is often like a life or death situation. They take it very seriously and a failure can almost seem like the end of the world. Without proper training in how to handle adversities in sports, such times can negatively influence the sports career of a child.

All parents find it challenging to teach their children how to handle themselves when they are faced with an adversity. As parents, the automatic response is often to protect a child from adversity, to keep them from the heartache of failure. However, the best way for your young athlete to rise to a high level of professionalism and success is to have a positive outlook on adversity, and even on times of failure.

In sports, adversities happen all the time—missing a field goal, getting disqualified because of a false start, or breaking a rule that cost an athlete the entire match. All of these situations and more happen on a regular basis. It is important to teach your child in advance about adversity that is bound to happen every now and then during their sports career. Then, when it happens, they have something to fall back on and help them maintain the proper perspective on the difficult event.

The real world of sports is intense and will be a big learning experience for your young athlete, but it can be taken in a positive or a negative way. My parents were always there for me during hard times. There were times when I had a pulled hamstring during a race when I was a young athlete starting my career. These times were very embarrassing and I often wanted to quit and not return to sports. If it wasn't for my parents who constantly motivated me to look past my current adversity, I wouldn't have been able to write this book today.

Thanks to my parents and their strength and training, they were able to keep my mind focused and help me become one of the best athletes in the world today. I faced many more adversities after high school and college, leading to my professional career. But if I hadn't been trained from the beginning to look past the present adversity, I wouldn't have been able to persevere onto higher levels in sports.

One of my most memorable and terrifying adversities in sports occurred during my professional career. If it wasn't for the training and reinforcements from my younger years in athletics about how to handle adversities, I wouldn't have been able to handle this devastating situation in my professional career.

In 2001, at a World Championship competition, during a hand-off exchange in the finals of a quarter mile relay representing the United States, I dropped the baton. The USA team was leading the race and I was the anchor leg to bring home the win. But during the exchange from the third-leg runner, I failed.

When the baton fell out of my hand, it quickly rolled into the infield. Realizing what had happened; I threw myself with lightening speed, grabbed the baton, and dashed back into the race. I ran as hard as I could to get back in the race. I was devastated and crying as I was running. I felt terrible about what had happened. I disappointed my teammates and my country. During the catch-up on my final leg in the relay, I was able to pass two runners.

When the race was over, I stood still and glanced in the stadium of thousands of people.

Tears came to my eyes immediately, not knowing how to react to what had just happened. I felt like I just let down my country. A minute later, I rushed off the track and out of the stadium in tears.

I then grabbed my clothes from the warm-up area and quickly caught a shuttle back to the hotel. The first thing I did was send an email to my mother explaining that I let down my country. My mother instantly sent a message saying that I need to keep my head up and that it was just a mistake.

I instantly realized that I was facing a sporting adversity that I had to get over before it consumed me. Yes, this was the first hand-off failure on the US Team, but I had to get over it. I had to move on and not lose sight of my goal in the sport.

It took me about a day to mentally recover after the incident. That was only possible because I knew how to handle adversity in my sports from training I received at a young age. If not for that, I might have been totally devastated for much longer. It wasn't new to me to 'drop the ball' during competitions. I've encountered numerous hurdles during my athletic career. But to keep going, one must put things in perspective.

I was also surprised and relieved that my USA team coach and other US officials were very proud of me. They were pleased that I did not give up and leave the baton on the infield. According to past histories, athletes that accidentally drop the baton during a highly competitive race would normally give up and stop running. Instead, I grabbed the stick and tried to make the best of the adversity. I give credit to my younger years of training how to handle adversities in sports when they come up.

For a young athlete to be fully prepared to handle adversities in their sport, they must be taught how. Parents have a major role in the process when they start early.

Winning

> *"This race is not just for the runner.*
> *Some of us walk while others*
> *barely crawl*
> *We make our way through spring*
> *and winter leaning on the strength*
> *that strengthens all"*
> *—Cindy Morgan, "Take My Life"*

Every athlete wants to win. It is just that simple. But not every one who runs will win. A child who is inspired to become a great athlete needs to learn how to strive for winning and still accept losing. It is essential for the child to learn that the true essence of winning is not always being a first-place "winner" all the time.

It is very difficult to teach a child that they cannot get everything they want in life, because all parents want their child to be happy. Every good parent has an innate desire to give their child everything that they need in order to be happy. Especially if you, as a parent, see your child striving so hard to train and become skilled at a sport, it could be difficult to accept that they will not always win.

This is also a very delicate learning process for the child, yet your positive and hopeful perspective, regardless of the exact outcome, can help them grow to accept with grace the times that they do not win. At this developmental stage of teaching your child how to deal with winning and accepting losing, you are preparing your young athlete to either be a great winner or a terrible loser. Every child is different and for some of them, it might take quite some time to teach them about how to handle wins and losses.

One way my parents guided me about winning when I was a young athlete was to constantly encourage me to be grateful for who I am. The more I recognized and was grateful for my abilities, the more I felt like a winner regardless of the outcome of my performance.

I hated to lose as a child, and my competitiveness was very intense from a young age. I pushed myself in everything I did at practice because I didn't want to get beat at the next competition. But there were times I got second, third, fourth, and even fifth place. It was painful every time and my parents knew it. Any time that my performance was not a win, my parents would tell me not to give up and to keep practicing hard.

Sports is about having fun and being the best you can be; as a parent, it is important to stress this concept to your child. The greatest athletes of all time love and enjoy their sport. You want your child to feel the same way too, so one day they will be a great athlete.

Never humiliate or threaten your child when they do not win. That will send a negative message to the child that will destroy their motivation to continue and do well in their sport. Never be too hard on your child to win a race or game. When a parent pressures a child that they must win, this steals the joy of the sport away from the child. This sends a negative message to the child that will forever resonate in their memory.

Sports is 90% mental, so if your child is not getting positive and motivating feedback from you, there is no telling how their performance in the sport could be negatively affected.

There are a tremendous amount of athletes in the world today who still have a hard time living with losses, so it is important to discuss in a positive manner the reality that there will be times they will lose. Teach them that winning and losing are all a part of the game.

Athletes who were not taught how to graciously accept both winning and losing will struggle immensely down the road, in their professional careers. Some are so afraid of losing that they unfortunately succumb to cheating by using illegal, performance-enhancing drugs. Eventually (but invariably) they get caught, and their names are blasted all over the media. For something like this to happen would be every parent's worst nightmare. To discover that your child's reputation is ruined forever, including the family's name would be very difficult to handle and overcome.

Teaching your young athlete how to win and lose gracefully will stay with them for a lifetime. They will be ready to become true athletes and their names will be remembered as great legends in their sport. In addition, this life lesson taught to your child will also be a valuable investment to help them with their daily lives as adults.

I was blessed to have parents who always encouraged me in a positive way, regardless of whether I won or not. This was very important to me because I loved my sport and I wanted to be remembered as a legendary sportswoman. This can be taught to your child too—that it's not about winning or losing. It's about the love of the game, the honing of their skills, and the enjoyment of participating in their much-loved sport, regardless of the outcome.

National Scholastic Indoor Championship. Focus and determination

Work

> *"Once a man has made a commitment to a way of life, he puts the greatest strength in the world behind it. Something we call 'heart power.' Once a man has made this commitment, nothing will stop him short of success."*
>
> —*Vince Lombardi*

To be a great athlete takes work, and a lot of it. There is no way around dedication and the willingness to work hard. Young athletes must be taught the powerful outcome of good old hard work. Because they are young, it will take practice to teach a child this important concept.

As I mentioned before, every athlete's desire is to win. Winning requires dedication, sacrifice, cooperation, and work. All of these must be taught as they are essential attributes for a young athlete's development. Parents play an important role in this process.

When I was a young athlete, I came to understand that a great work ethic was important for me if I wanted to succeed. Your child's work ethic can be molded if you are consistent in reinforcing good behavior and correcting unhealthy conduct.

For example, if you notice you child complaining about their times of practice—that it's too hard, or they have to get up too early or that they don't feel like it today—you can remind your child of the commitment they made to be a great athlete. This sounds very simple to do, but it is not easy. Most young athletes understand that to be the best they must work hard, and if you reinforce this, they will learn to be persistent with their training and honing their skills.

Success is the result of constant and relentless dedication. One way my parents constantly motivated me to work hard was to reward me. Children love to get a reward of some kind for doing something good; it shows that their behavior was noticed and appreciated. I remember receiving extra money allowances for good work ethics and it always worked. I was proud of myself every time I was rewarded for my dedication to work hard and it increased my desire to continue honing my work ethic.

When I entered high school and joined the track team, I was not the best runner. Many girls were faster than me. However, my ambition was to be the best not only in high school but the best in the nation among high school athletes. To make my dreams come true, I knew I had to work harder than the rest of the athletes.

At our practices we trained as a group so we were getting the same amount of training and getting faster together. To be the best I realized that I had to do something extra. I then committed myself to extra training on Sundays.

My hard work quickly paid off. By my junior and senior year in high school, I was a two-time national high school champion and was ranked number in the United States in my event among high school athletes. Hard work does pay off, and with this concept taught to your child, they too can do phenomenal things in their sport. Just believe it can be done and your young athlete will feel your positive energy—and do it!

One main message about working hard is that there is no substitute for it. Working halfway will not cut it, and your child needs to understand this. If this is not properly taught and understood, a poorly developed work ethic can follow your child for the rest of his or her life. One of the major reasons why parents like to enrol their children in sport activities at a young age is because it trains the child in self-discipline and ambition. A disciplined lifestyle taught from a young age will help them be successful adults and as they progress through life.

Many athletes, at various levels in their sport careers, have a very poor work ethic. We see this all the time in the media. These people range from young to professional athletes. As a result of a poor work ethic, some of these athletes who struggle to be successful in their sport look for a shortcut and use illegal, performance-enhancing drugs to try to get to the top. As I mentioned before, there is no substitute for working hard, and when an athlete decides to cheat, they will lose.

Not only will a cheating athlete lose, but you will suffer too. It is impossible to know exactly what your child will achieve in their sport later on in their career, but your child stands a much better chance in refusing to cheat if they are trained at an early age about honestly working hard to reach any level of success. As you can see, it is important to train children correctly how to work hard if they want to be champions in their sport.

Part Two

There are many outstanding coaches in the sports industry. Moreover, there are some coaches who are well known for their expertise in training their athletes to achieve great things in their sport. Some coaches are so talented that they created several legendary world-class athletes during their coaching career.

A coach is one of the most important people in your child's sporting career. As a parent, you must take an active role in selecting the right coach. This coach could be temporary or long-term, but regardless of how long you plan to use a coach, selecting the right one is imperative. The final selection will have a strong impact on your child's sports career forever. So it definitely pays to find the right coach for your young athlete.

Although, as I mentioned, there are exemplary coaches, on the other hand—just like in every area of life—there are coaches in various levels of each sport who don't have their athletes' best interests at heart. You can come to recognize them, but you must do your homework. Otherwise, ending up with the wrong coach can be a disastrous nightmare for your young athlete and you as well.

I've been blessed with phenomenal coaches who trained me through high school, others during college and in my professional years. My coaches had the gift of bringing out the best in me during practices and competition. Each coach had a different style of coaching, but the aim was the same: to ensure I was prepared to compete at my best.

The sports industry is a very lucrative business, and many people who enjoy sports often want to be a part of the action in some way. There are literally thousands of careers in sports, with billions of dollars to go around for everybody involved. Just like with any other business, there will always be bad apples who cause problems and there will be people who are not loyal or honest in what they do.

Choosing the right coach for your young champion-to-be is the central theme of this book, so we will take some time right here to understand the coaching business. This will help you understand why coaches can be so powerful and how they fit into the overall sports picture. You will learn about the murky waters and some of their dark secrets.

The Sports Coaching Business

In this chapter I'm going to tell you a little about the coaching business. It's important to understand what motivates coaches, the good and the bad. Most just want to see the young people achieve their potential and succeed in their chosen sport. A few are driven by more selfish forces. I'll tell you a little about the coaching profession, about the levels of coaching I went through, and then about the ways in which coaches make money.

But first, the obvious question:

Why use Coaches?

Coaches are necessary to assess an athlete and/or team's capability and improve it, maximizing the chance of winning. The coaching advice can range from diet to the finer points of a high jumper's approach run, from the right weight training regime to the best spikes for a given surface and weather conditions.

They see the athlete perform, look for weaknesses that can be worked on and improved, strengths that can be built on. Is the runner better at 200 meters or would longer distance races suit the runner better? Would the boxer win more by moving up a weight category, or down? The coach provides this expert input based on detailed knowledge of the sport.

The coach will work with the athlete to make sure that their training regime brings them to the peak of their performance capability juts at the right time for a major competition.

The leverage that a good coach can provide to an athlete's performance is massive.

That's why we use coaches.

How are Coaches Qualified?

Most coaches will have been athletes themselves in that sport, though they may not necessarily have won the top honors—in fact that is usually not the case. That does not mean that they do not make good coaches. Being a coach is about technical knowledge, about managing people and about motivating their athletes. The best coaches have all three attributes in great depth, able to analyze an athlete's performance, judge how they are performing relative to their capability at that time and how they can improve both their performance and capability, and pushing them to their limit at the right time.

Sports people who have the strongest desire to win have to have a degree of aggression to tackle their individual pain barriers and push through the limits their individual performance envelopes to attain higher performance goals. A good coach is able to build that aggression in his athletes and help them close out all other pressures and focus the aggression on their performance. This is a great coaching skill, and not all coaches have it in depth.

So, those are the skills that a coach needs, and provides the basic qualifications.

Some coaches will have studied at college and hold a BSC (Bachelor of Sports Coaching) or BSS degree (Bachelor of Sports Science). Indeed, many athletes will themselves have earned the BSS qualification (as I did myself). The well-regarded US Sports Academy offers certification course for Coaches as does the US Track and Field and Cross Country Coaches Association (couldn't they have come up with a shorter name)?

US Collegiate Sports associations have a structure for registering coaches and setting basic professional (and ethical) standards, to ensure that the good name of the particular sport is not damaged by any unethical behaviour on the part of coaches. For example, the American Football Coaches Association was set up in 1922—one of the first. Its Code of Ethics includes a section on 'Responsibilities to Players'. The schemes are also meant to ensure that there is at least a minimum standard of capability in the three basic coaching attributes.

Professional coaching is less structured and organized. In only a few sports do aspiring coaches may have to attend courses and even pass exams to demonstrate that they are competent and to gain their coaching 'badge'.

USA Football (the sport's governing body) has a long list of ethical standards that coaches should stick to.

That sets the ideal structure within a sport, and may be mandatory if the US governing sports body is to be recognized internationally and its athletes be allowed to compete in official international competitions.

Improper, unethical and even criminal behaviour by a coach which is judged to have brought his (or her) sport into disrepute can result in loss of the coaching license. That is the ideal, but it doesn't apply across all sports. The reality is that the temptations are so powerful that a minority of coaches do break the rules and encourage the athletes they coach to do so as well. I've met a few! Sadly, some coaches are never caught and shamed.

Successful coaches may become better known (and rewarded) than the athletes or players they coach, with radio and TV programmes of their own and a face which effectively becomes that of the team. Thankfully this is not the case at the lower levels of sport, where your own budding champion needs a coach.

In May 2012, Forbes Magazine reported that two top NFL coaches earned more than $7 million a year each, and that's without all the sponsorships and other tie-ins that they enjoy. These guys are the leaders of their profession and have the results to prove it, and I'm not for a minute implying that they didn't achieve that in any way other than ethically. The point is that with the potential for money on that scale, there will always be people who are tempted. Every barrel has one or two rotten apples.

Eight of the highest paid sports coaches in the US work in the NFL.

Growth of the Sports Coaching Industry

> 'You shall remember the Lord your God, for it is He who give you power to get wealth.
> —Deuteronomy 8:18—in the Holy Bible, New Kings James Version

The post 'baby boomer' generation of parents—that's you—is well-informed and concerned about increased obesity and lack of fitness in their children. This concern is increasing demand for coaching services. That extra need is on top of existing demand. Sports camps are multiplying and demand for coaches is growing quickly. And that growth is certain to mean a drop in standards. As if finding the best coach for your child wasn't hard enough already!

The US sports coaching industry has been estimated to generate $2.4 billion dollars a year, out of a total $400 billion sports industry total. That's a big number in anybody's bank account.

College competition for the best coaching talent drives up coaching rewards in the most lucrative sports such as football and basketball.

So, rewards are increasing and demand is increasing. That's all sure to make it harder to find the right sports coach and add a few more rotten apples to the barrel. Sport is big business and the best talent is rewarded well, but with increased demand the temptation to take short cuts to success which was ever present, is now growing.

The Coach's Responsibilities

When you choose a coach, you need to understand what the coach's responsibilities are to your adolescent champion-to-be. I'm going to tell you about those responsibilities because understanding them will help you ask deeper questions when you come to interviewing a prospective coach, and help you judge which coach to trust.

The responsibilities of a coach are linked to their ethical code and to their employer (if working at a high school, for example).

Here's an extract from the ICCE Model Code (International Council for Coach Education), which is used as a guide for sports associations to create their own code. Whether it's athletics or basketball, hockey or handball, the basic principles are the same.

Principles/ Values	Focus
Competence	Coach education
Trustworthiness	Keep rules of confidentiality; Inspire trust in own athletes
Respect	Athletes, decisions, rules, promises, commitments, privacy
Fairness	Fair-play; same opportunities for each athlete; No use of illegal substances and methods
Caring	For athletes and animals; well-being of physical and emotional state of athletes
Integrity	Stay true to own values and actions; Act as a role model
Responsibility	For development of the athlete; For own development as a coach

Individual sports usually have more detailed codes—for example banning smoking in the presence of athletes, and so on—but generally they are based on these principles.

Responsibility is only one part of this, yet it is very far reaching, and its aspects go beyond sport—they can include a pastoral aspect. Have you ever heard the phrase 'in loco parentis'? No? Well it's Latin and nothing to do with crazy parents—though sometimes with all the traveling you do ask yourself the question!

What this phrase means is 'in place of the parent', and you can see from the ethics guidelines above that coaches should care for their young athletes and act as role models. As I said earlier, young athletes have very limited life experience. So, they rely on and trust their coaches and because of this they will tend to believe everything the coach tells them. That trust can be abused by unscrupulous coaches.

Of course for a budding athlete, ball player or boxer to excel, they have to have a very strong desire to win, and I talk about this in depth elsewhere. Now, imagine that this desire to win is like a powerful force—which it is. The momentum of an automobile is tremendous at just 20 mph, yet a child can change its direction with just a little tweak of the steering wheel. So it is with coaches and young athletes.

With a very powerfully motivated young sportsperson, that momentum—desire to win—can be unstoppable, but it can also be easily diverted. It doesn't take much persuasion from a trusted coach to change the direction of that desire and send an impressionable young athlete off the straight and narrow, down the dark, illegal road to success. Judo is another illustration. This Olympic fighting sport uses the strength and weight of the opponent against them to gain a fall. Don't let your son become the fall-guy when the coach uses your son's competitive weight to misguide him.

There are codes of ethics for athletics and other sports, and it is a great idea to talk through them with your child so that they understand that winning is only winning if it's done legally. It's like a school exam—children who cheat are really only cheating themselves. Most cheats get found out sooner or later but their character is damaged because the idea of cheating is acceptable. It is a universal principle in life as well as in sport.

The main point here is that all good coaches operate under an ethical code. The bad coaches ignore such codes.

For your youngster's sake, you need to know how to recognize bad coaches.

Levels of Coaching

My parents were involved in sports when they were young, so they both wished the same for me. So I got involved too, with a youth athletic summer track team called Glenarden Track Club. That is the first step on the coaching ladder, when a very young athlete becomes involved with the coaching business, usually through a club.

Glenarden is one of many summer track clubs for kids from Bandits (7-8 years old) to Youths

(17-18 years old). This summer track club is one of many all over the United States that coach children without charging the parents a fee. My parents and other parents did not have to pay the coaches a fee to coach us. The only costs to the parents were for traveling and hotel lodging when the team traveled out of state—these were qualifying state and national competitions with other summer track teams from across the United States.

All sports have a similar approach. It helps young sports people and it's healthy for them even if they don't go on to become high performers. It also helps an individual sport find its stars of the future, whether it is football, athletics, swimming and even skateboarding. It's also a great social arena for youngsters—and even their parents!

This is how I initially established myself in athletics in the United States. It was through a summer track team that I participated in during the summer months when school was out. It was fun because I was able to practice my running skills, meet other young athletes, and travel. My parents enjoyed it too because they got the chance to travel, watch the competitions and meet other like-minded parents.

In the high school coaching business, the majority of the coaches are teachers and they have an additional responsibility of coaching a sport. These can be basketball, soccer, cheerleading, athletes and many others. They do not get any additional pay from parents to coach their children in sports. If a student shows above average sporting ability though, their encouragement and support is very valuable. That is the second level. Next comes the college level.

In college, the structure is similar except that most collegiate coaches are strictly the head or assistant coach for the designated sport. Coaching at this level is starting to become very serious for the student—and for the coach. This is because a collegiate coach can coach an athlete to be a professional on the side, for a fee. I did. However, there is an important rule that these collegiate coaches must follow: the collegiate athletes can not train with the professional athletes at the same time. At the University of Texas at Austin, this was the case when I was there.

The next level is full professional coaching. After my collegiate career at the University of Texas at Austin, I hired my collegiate coach as my professional coach. Beverly Kearney was already a well established Olympic coach who had many famous athletes under her guidance. I wanted to be a part of her professional team. So I joined it.

Before joining such a team there is a process to go through and this can be challenging. The real world is rearing its business head and an aspiring professional sportsperson has to examine their motivation and commitment very seriously.

In my case, I had to sign with a professional sponsor. At the time, it was Adidas America. It was a very exciting time for me because I was running well and ranked in the top 8 in the world in the 400m coming out of college. With my contract with Adidas America, I was able to commit to a payment agreement to pay my coach. I was lucky, but it is not so easy for everyone, and some dreams could be shattered at this time.

We are now at the full professional level, though even here some athletes might still have to hold down a regular job.

But it's not only the athletes who compete. Coaches have their own competitions too, maybe not so obvious at first, but they exist. Some coaching federations make Coach of the Season or Coach of the Year awards. These awards help coaches command higher fee levels. As they say, it pays to advertise and for the top coaches this is another great point for the resumé. Everyone expects to pay more for the best!

How Coaches Make Money

Sports coaches have a wide number of ways of making money from their sport. Many have a salary from the college or sports team they *work for, and it goes without saying that the most successful coaches make the most money. However, at the professional level the money available varies from sport to sport.*

In the US, the highest paid sports coaches work in Football, with earnings approaching $10 million a year. That includes salary and other income from sponsors, endorsements and even radio and TV shows. Autos may be provided for them to use and free upgrades on airplane travel are quite common. There are plenty of other 'perks' too.

These are the exceptions but nevertheless many coaches earn well in excess of 6 figures. Contrast that with an average high school coaching salary of about $32,000 a year.

Many coaches have their rewards linked to their successes—perhaps a Major League Title or World Championship at the top level. The top coaches may also hold equity in a team, owning some of the shares and earning some of the profits. It's not common but it does happen.

I mentioned endorsements, but there are hidden ones too. For major sports teams, the team owners and management may be approached for an official endorsement for equipment or other items, but the coach wields power and can influence that decision.

So, there is plenty of money around, and the biggest rewards are at the top. To get there a coach needs success from the athletes he or she coaches—medals, championships, records and even press coverage. Whether it's in the high jump or 100 meters freestyle swimming, football or hockey, success raises the coach's status and potential earnings.

One thing they don't want is scandal, but sadly, too many take the risk.

Coaches need leverage to get in to the 'big league'. If your adolescent son or daughter has even a modest chance of success, but is failing to hit the tape first then the temptation for an unscrupulous coach might be too great. The coach might see your hopeful young champion as a way of advancing his (or her) own coaching career. Your teenage hopeful will be 'leverage'.

Then, the dangers of performance enhancers and overtraining become very real.

Dark Secret

Unethical coaches and managers approach athletes to use drugs so they can make a profit.

During my professional career I was approached by a respected coach who tried to persuade me to use performance enhancing drugs to win more races because everyone was doing it. The coach said that if all the connections were provided, the profit would be fifty percent of all my income from my races.

So coaches and managers are only in the illegal sports drug business not because they like the athlete and they care—it is just to make a profit for themselves.

Choosing a Coach

You can see from the huge numbers I quoted earlier that the coaching business is awash with money. That means that there is plenty of temptation out there in the real sports world for both coaches and athletes. Fortunately, the bad eggs are few and far between but you have to learn how to make sure you select the good eggs. It's not quite as easy as spinning an egg on the table-top!

> *'Keep your face to the sunshine, and you will not see the shadows.'*
> *—Helen Keller*

That is a beautifully positive statement, but unfortunately we do have to face the shadows from time to time.

Knowing Which Coach to Trust

Throughout my career, I've discovered many coaches who went beyond ethical means to get their athletes ready for competition, regardless of the potential consequences being banned or suspended. Some coaches would go so far as to introduce dangerous and illegal, performance-enhancing drugs to their athletes to allow them to have an extra "edge" during competitions. The coaches that take this risk have one thing on their mind—money. And they will use and manipulate any athlete who is mentally too weak to resist. Many famous athletes get in serious trouble because they violate the pure ethics of sport; the reputation of the coach is often negatively affected as well. Most times, the athlete had good intentions, but because of bad influence their future in sports is tarnished forever.

Every athlete deserves to know that they can trust their coach. A coach is like a pilot of a commercial plane with passengers in it. We purchase our airplane tickets for a seat in the aircraft so we can get to our destination. When we hand our boarding pass to the flight attendant, we never stop and question if the pilot is a certified and experienced to fly the plane. We get on board and enjoy our flight knowing that we will get to our destination.

A coach is considered qualified and capable to direct the lives of people to improve their athletic abilities. They are considered visionaries who have the mastery to see deep inside the soul of their athletes and tap into a sea of abilities that is unseen to the athlete. Coaches are like skilled psychologists; they are adept in knowing exactly how to get their athletes to visualize and think during practices and competitions. Coaches are also like cheerleaders; they inspire and keep their athletes moving in the direction they want them to go.

So imagine for a moment sending your child off to a dishonest coach with these phenomenal abilities I just listed. How would you feel if you found out after it was too late that your young athlete is under the wing of a coach that does not have your child's best interest at heart? What if you send your child off to a coach that is only in the sports business to tap into some of the billions of dollars floating around in the sports business?

This can be avoided with some simple steps on your part. For your future athlete to be safe and have a promising career, you need to research diligently to find the best coach for your child. To start, I would suggest that you get more involved and thoroughly examine all the coaches your child is interested in.

Do not rush, because it will take time and lots of patience.

It is well worth it though!

The Power of Intuitive Involvement

My parents were very active in my selection for the right coach when I was a young athlete in elementary school. The first step they took was to check out all the good track teams in our community. We quickly realized that there were too many coaches to pick from. Some were well recognized and others were not. Some had a team of over 200 athletes; others had only 5 athletes.

My parents soon realized that they needed to use their intuition and not just blindly select any old coach. I remember my mother investigating various coaches from several summer clubs. A lot of them had successful athletes on their teams, but we wanted to make sure we selected the one that gave us the best vibes.

To our surprise, some coaches of the summer teams were very selective themselves. They wanted me to take individual event tests and the whole nine yards to make sure I was the kind of athlete they wanted to coach. That's a good sign to look out for. That was ok with me too, because I found the event tests a lot of fun.

The secret to your search for the right coach is to use your intuition. One misjudgement during this important process can lead to the beginning of a dark sea of trouble. It can be a nightmare for you and your young athlete.

To avoid this, get involved and be inquisitive in your child's sports life. It sounds simple, but when you see the vast number of young athletes showing up on the news with public embarrassment due to having the wrong coach, this hits home.

Getting involved and inquisitive should not be considered an arduous process. The best way to know the truth about a coach is to ask as many questions as possible. Just realize that this person could possibly be spending a lot of time with your child throughout their career in sports. Remember what I said about a pastoral aspect? What values do they have? What methods do they use to inspire and motivate their athletes? What kind of relationship do they have with the athletes that they coach? Are they planning on retiring soon? Is coaching their passion, or just a job?

Define what is important to you and your child as far as values or methods, and don't be afraid to ask a prospective coach about it.

If your child is not in high school and is planning to use a coach to get ready for summer leagues or other extra-curricular activities, research as many coaches in your area as possible. You can do this by checking with your local YMCA, community youth clubs, newspaper, phone book, or other parents with kids in sports. Once you have at least five to ten leads to coaches, call each of them, introduce yourself and tell them what your intentions are for child. Then ask for a time to meet with the coach and observe his team.

I highly recommend that you and your young athlete meet with each coach at the facility where they train their athletes. That way you can see the coach in action during a practice and observe how he or she interacts with the athletes. This is so important because your first vibes about the coach and the environment is often your best advisor. Don't second guess your intuition at this point. Moreover, your child will often know if that's the right place for them so their input is vitally important.

While you and your child are observing the coach and the other athletes, take the time to ask other parents and athletes what they think about the coach. This is another proactive way to get information. By doing this, you will sense if the other parents are happy or uncomfortable. Don't be afraid to ask questions and get inquisitive; other parents understand that this is an important decision for you and your child to make.

In addition to observing, pay close attention to the athlete's interaction with the coach. Watch very closely how the best and the average athletes respond to the coach. Be the detective. When you are observing, try to visualize your child on the team. If you feel excited about what you sense, then that's a good sign. If not, then it's not.

When you meet with the coach face to face, ask as many questions as needed. And listen keenly, not only with your ears, but with your vibes. Ask questions that focus on how long he or she has been coaching young athletes and what have they accomplished during their career. This will give you a sense of the coach's experience.

Check to see how often the team attends competitions and so forth. But the main focus is to get the coach talking and expressing how they're passionate about working with young athletes. The more questions you ask is the more you'll know about the coach's genuineness. A coach with their athletes' best interests at heart will go beyond measure to express and show why he or she is the best for your child.

How to Research a Coach

To research a coach properly takes time. Taking the time to find out about all the coaches that you are interested in is very important. It is a mistake to accept any offer that sounds good. Even if a coach produced great or famous athletes, how would you know if that is the right coach for your young athlete?

It is important to know the coach's style and modes of operation. When I was a younger athlete, my parents and I asked other athletes and coaches about the particular coach that we were interested in. Do not be afraid to ask questions regardless of how stupid or irrelevant you think those questions might be. The more you know about a coach and his or her style, the better.

To effectively research a coach, start off by having an initial face-to-face interview as well as a follow-up to that interview. Get inquisitive. This is your child's future, so don't be complacent. Ask questions about how he or she deals with parents—and assess how the coach is dealing *with you. A coach who believes their athletes' progress and future are important will always feel accountable to the parents of that athlete. So get involved!*

Associate yourself with other parents whose children are being trained by the same coach. If you do not have connections to other parents with a coach that you are interviewing, ask the coach for references and other staff members that will know about his or her history and character. The more people you talk to, the better.

Another way to discover the right coach is by conducting research on the internet. You never know what you will find! There is so much information online that it is almost impossible not to find what you want. The internet is a great place to find information about coaches, their current and past athletes, news reports, statistical reports, performance, and even information about their character and conduct. All these and more are very important in making a decision for your child's future with a sport coach.

Another source to research about a coach is to inquire at your child's main sports' federation. It may be in football, basketball, swimming, softball, soccer, track and field, or cycling. All sports federations have pertinent information about active coaches in the United States.

If a coach is actively involved in a nationally recognized federation of your child's sport, that's a positive sign. It means that the coach is serious about contributing to that particular sport in a positive way, and wants to make a great impact to the sport by being a contributor. I've always admired coaches that are involved in making my sport better. That says a lot about a coach's beliefs.

Contracts with Coaches

Depending on a coach's level of experience and expertise in a particular sport, some coaches require a contract, a legal agreement between coach and athlete. In this rapidly evolving world of sports, this is not uncommon. Just like any binding contract, it is important to be familiar with all the intricate details of the written agreement and the coach.

Never agree to sign with a coach unless you are fully aware of everything in question. I recommend hiring a lawyer that specializes in sports law to go over all contracts and binding agreements before you and your athlete commit. A lawyer can recognize anything in the contract that is not in your athlete's best interest. It is best to be cautious at this point.

I've seen many athletes and their coach get into major disputes about contracts after they have been signed. Lawsuits galore are inevitable when both parties are no longer in agreement. This can be avoided simply by the athlete and their parents knowing what their coach's value systems are. Not knowing what you truly want, and failing to get legal advice, will most likely result in problems happening between the athlete and the coach.

In the Appendix you will find a sample Contract to give you an idea what they look like, although there can be big variations. It is a guideline only, not to be relied on legally.

Part Three

The Importance of Finding the Right College

If your child is an athlete in high school and he or she is getting ready to select a college to continue their career in sport, this is when you as the parent must be very investigative and focused. This is one of the most challenging times for most star athletes, especially if they were successful enough to get an athletic scholarship. Not only is this a very challenging time for both you and your young athlete, but it can also be an exciting process.

The college coach will play a key part in the future of your young athlete.

There are hundreds of colleges and universities with athletic programs all over the United States. To select the right one for your young athlete, it is best to know exactly what both of you want.

During my senior year in high school, I was overwhelmed by the enormous number of universities that wanted me to attend their school. The letters were coming in so frequently that I can remember counting about five letters a day. I definitely needed help and am grateful that my parents decided to be very proactive during the selection process.

In my heart I knew exactly what I wanted. My first priority was to attend a university that had a very successful athletic program. I thought the best track team in the country would be beneficial because I dreamed of being a professional athlete even after college. Not only did I want the best athletic program, but I also wanted the best academic program. I didn't know if that was possible, but I was determined to find and accept the offer of the school of my dreams.

My parents, however, had a slightly different desire for me. They wanted me to go to a university that had a very strong academic and athletic program, but one that was close to home. This made the search for that perfect school more complicated.

Every athlete, including your child, is unique. An athlete's desire can range from wanting to be a collegiate athlete to a professional athlete, or from an Olympic athlete to a world record holder. Whatever your young athlete's desires are, have faith that they can achieve it. It makes a big difference during the process when a parent can help to make their child's dreams come true. You are the best person in the world to assist your young athlete to reach the stars.

My parents knew how important my dreams were to me, so they both took the research process seriously. During our extensive search, we were able to narrow down the options to two schools.

To even get to this stage effectively, I recommend that you make a list of what's most important to you and your child. Then simply use the process of elimination. You will be surprised how quickly you'll be able to remove the schools that don't fit your interests.

After you and your young athlete select a college, it is best to arrange a campus visit. Normally, college coaches will gladly agree for an athlete to visit their school. Most college coaches want you to see the campus and sport facilities so the athlete can see 'in living color' what they have to offer. This is an important step because it will enable you and your child to know for sure if that's the right environment and coach. You may even discover the dream school for your child.

To make the decision process easier, I decided it was best to bring a parent with me to my first college visit. My mother was excited and anxious to come. Athletes might usually go on a college visit alone, since they are the primary person that will be attending the school for the next four years. But both my parents and I thought it would be more proactive to make it a family decision.

Bringing a parent was one of the best decisions I've ever made in the sense that it affected my athletic career in a positive way. On my first visit to the University of Texas, my mother and I extensively tested our vibes to make sure the school was the right fit. The university had the best collegiate athletic program in the nation and was ranked in the top 20 academically among Ivy League schools. The only disappointment for my parents and I was that Texas was more than a 24-hour drive from my parents' home.

The purpose of your visit should be to ask as many questions as possible in person as well as to get a feel for the school. The questions that are most important for you to ask will vary, depending on the goals of your young athlete. The main focus should be to figure out if 'you have the right coach to meet the athlete's goals. The academic program could be exactly what you want, but if you go with the wrong coach, this can cause an extreme conflict. Be sure that you and your young adult balance all your desires properly.

My mother and I had so much fun with the coach and the athletic team that we both knew right away the University of Texas was the right school for me, despite the distance. The coach was one of the best in the world and had an exceptional, world-recognized talent in training future Olympic athletes. All her Olympic athletes were gold, silver, or bronze medallists.

That visit to the University of Texas and meeting with the coach and other staff members even now stands out in my mind as a special time. My mother and I wouldn't have experienced what we did if we weren't physically there. Having my mother with me during that visit helped me tremendously in making the right decision, to attend that school.

Don't be afraid to visit and get a feel of colleges with your young athlete. It will help set the tone for your child's future career. The college coaches and the other staff members will appreciate how involved you are as a parent in your child's life.

The Importance of Parental Attendance

Getting involved in your athlete's sport career can be very rewarding to you and your child. Not only will you enable your child to be the best that they can be in their sport, but you can also watch them progress and, over time, turn into superstars.

Attending as many games, practices, and any other important events as possible will also keep you alert of what is evolving in your child's life. This is so important. You never know what you'll discover when you get involved. When a parent is involved and in attendance of the majority of their athlete's' sports life, this can also deter possible unseen harmful things and situations that may have an effect on your child.

My parents attended over ninety percent of all my races from the time I participated in games during my youth all the way to my professional career in athletics. They both considered their presence important at my sporting events because they knew it would motivate me to perform at my best if they were among the spectators. My parents also knew that attending my practices and sport events would send a positive message to my coaches and teammates.

This suggestion about parents' attendance may seem like an ordinary point but it is extraordinary in paving the way for your young athlete's success in their sport. From years of experience as a young athlete leading up to a professional career, I've seen athletes go down a 'hole in the ground'—or worse—because they got negatively influenced to do things unethical to themselves and their sport, such as getting involved and convinced to use performance-enhancing drugs.

It is far easies for a coach or teammate to manipulate and persuade a weak-minded athlete to do things unethical to themselves and their sport if their parents are not actively involved. Young athletes, and even professionals in sports, are influenced by coaches they trust every day.

During my career, I've seen so many athletes regret getting involved with the wrong people in their career. This does not necessarily mean their coaches, but various people that they interact with in their sports world. These could be teammates, therapists, or even sport doctors who influence an athlete to go the unethical route and jeopardize their entire sports career. It happens way too often.

Therefore, never get complacent to think that your young athlete will be alright if you don't attend their practices, games, team functions, etc. Never put your guard down. Never put all your trust and responsibility on your child's coaches either. Be involved in every aspect of your child's career in sports.

The main point of attendance is obviously not only to support your young athlete, but to protect them from the possible things and people that can influence your child to do wrong. To be a part of everything that your child is participating in is almost unattainable, but do understand that showing your face and taking part on a regular basis will have a positive effect on your young athlete's' future.

**Powerful block start at High School Nationals
Scholastic finals**

The Power of Communication

In all relationships—be it in personal, family, or business—communication is the main ingredient for survival. Most people know this in theory, but unfortunately, the majority struggle with this key component. In sports, especially important for you as a parent, it is important that you invest a lot of your time in communication.

The benefits of having a strong, open and communicative relationship with your young athlete and their coaches are enormous. Parents are advised to take this very seriously as it can also lead your child to a greater level of success in their sport.

Without good communication with your child, you could be inadvertently setting up your athlete for failures in the future. This is possible if a parent is not actively being inquisitive about the welfare of their young athlete.

Asking your child questions about how they feel about their practices, progression in their performance, games and events, and their relationship with their coach and teammates can be very revealing. Just taking the time to find out how your child feels and letting them express how they feel will keep you up to date. Never be afraid to ask as many questions as possible.

Having a strong communication relationship with your child's coach, regardless of whether your young athlete is a preschooler or a professional *athlete, is probably one of the best steps you can take as a parent. This is important because the coaches are the biggest influence in your young athlete's sport career. Some of these coaches could be actively involved in the development of your child's career in sports for many years. So it is important to really get to know the coach and build strong communication with him or her.*

Throughout my career, my parents were always actively involved with my coaches and me. I can remember them often asking me intricate questions about my training and my competitions. There were many times my parents and I would talk for hours at dinner with the rest of the family to get my thoughts and opinions about my progress in my sport. They would also ask me questions about my views about current sport issues that were in the news at the time. I enjoyed the extensive conversations with my parents and the rest of my family because it made me feel that they cared about me and my sport.

It was also great for my parents because they wanted to keep me balanced. They didn't want me to lose my ethical values about myself. This factor was important to my parents and the rest of my family. They were often disgusted to hear that an athlete that they admired got caught up in negative influences and went down the wrong path. They were being good parents of a young athlete, and I appreciated them for leading me in the right and prosperous direction in my sport.

The strong foundation I received as child enabled me to withstand negative influences in all aspects of my life. Without the inquisitiveness and training of my parents, I am not sure where I would've end up in my sports career. Many positive young athletes who were raised in good homes and had great role-model parents unfortunately still bit the bait of destruction in their sport or in other areas of their life. Nobody is perfect—even athletes—but I believe that strong communication with a parent or a guardian in a young athlete's life will have a positive impact when the tests of time arrive.

Communication between parent and coach is second in importance, coming right after your communication with your child. This basically puts your coach in the mindset that you are 'the parent' and you are in actively involved in the athletic development of your child. This sends a positive statement that will not only attract more positive situations but also discourage any possible evasiveness preconceived by the coach to do harm to your child.

It doesn't matter if your child is in professional sports or not; whatever your situation is, make a concerted effort to have a strong relationship with these coaches.

A parent's power of establishing and maintaining strong communication with their child's coach is one of the surest protections that you can have. Too many parents don't get involved or they are timid. They put all their trust and power in the coaches, hoping that everything would be alright and their child would still reach the top.

Too many parents give coaches tremendous power by not communicating with them on a regular basis. Not only is this ineffective approach dangerous and destructive, but the young athlete will adopt this mindset too and will automatically exclude you from important issues with their coach. Dedicating your time to have strong communication with your child's coach is a mindset that must be realized and practiced regularly.

An example of a parent having strong communication with one of my past coaches was during a time I was having a problem with the property management company of my new apartment. I had moved out on my own for the first time to get ready for a new phase in my professional career.

At the time, I had a problem with my apartment and I needed to change it, but the apartment's management did not see a problem. I was too bashful to call my new coach about the problem, so I called my mother to get her advice about how to handle the problem. My mother did not hesitate one second to call the new coach about the problem I was having. The coach then called the apartment's management and worked out a deal with them so I could get another place.

My parents also would frequently call my coaches on the phone to check on my progress (in their opinion rather than my own) and they attended team dinners with the coaches to keep the relationship of communication going.

There were also times my parents would sit with the coaches during important events, which also builds that trust of constant communication and involvement. My parents and I sometimes visited my coaches at their homes or invited them to dinner, which is also a way of establishing a strong communication level with a coach.

In short, do not be afraid or too timid to get involved. This is your child's future, regardless of where they are in their sport right now. You will discover more information about all involved only if you delve into your fears of getting inquisitive.

The Power of Stopovers

Another way of figuring out if a coach is the right fit for your child is simply visiting on a random basis. This might sound disreputable and outrageous, but you would be surprised how effective this suggestion is to make sure your young athlete's coach is in compliance. It is a way of getting involved, but visiting is also a way of discretely discovering any unknown information about a coach's mode of operation and conduct.

I'll give you an example of how important random visits are in maintaining a healthy balance for your young athlete's future in sports. In every area of our society, there are often "extra eyes" that are unseen to make sure we are safe and in compliance with the law. For example, the IRS is to make sure America's citizens all pay taxes; in addition, the Secret Service is to protect and investigate the welfare of the highest leaders of this country. You might occasionally need to be those "extra eyes" to guide your young athlete to the top.

When I was a professional athlete, most of my teammates seldom saw their parents. My parents frequently made trips to observe how my transitions unfolded and how I was doing. I didn't mind because I knew that my parents genuinely wanted the best for me.

The Importance of Sacrifice

As I mentioned already, my parents got involved with my career by taking the time to attend many of my sporting events. They drove over eight hours, to another state, just to watch me compete. They were really involved.

I remember my mother coming alone at times to watch me compete. My dad could not come because of his work, but my mother found the time to travel all the way to California to watch me compete. Her presence alone was a statement. It spells support and strength to a child, even when that child has grown up.

The young athletes who are not fortunate enough to get the support of their parents and family members are more vulnerable to get taken advantage of by the system. I've seen many subtle coaches manipulate their athletes and destroy their future. Don't let this happen to your young superstar.

Everywhere I travelled, my parents tried their hardest to be there to give me ultimate support. And with that support, I was unbeatable. As a result, any crookedness that might have tried to influence me could not get through because of the lessons my parents taught me and reinforced through their love and sacrifice.

Leading the pack at Penn Relays.
My parents are in the crowd cheering

Part Four

THE SECRET WORLD OF PERFORMANCE-ENHANCING DRUGS

Dark Secret

The illegal sports drug business is huge, but much of the research is legal.

It starts with the pharmaceutical companies which research and produce the performance enhancing drugs, flows through the distributors and out on to the track.

In every area of our planet, there are people in the business of manipulating people to get the upper hand, not caring about the effects that they have on others. That's a major concern you must realize you have as a parent with a child or children in sports.

For example, performance-enhancing drugs are extremely prevalent in sports. Some coaches are in the business of enhancing the performances of their athletes by supplying drugs to quickly bring an athlete to the highest level in competition.

From the beginning of sports, there has always been cheating. And in most cases where drugs are involved, the cheaters get caught, either during their sport career, or due to the body's later reaction to the drugs. This is a very common pattern. It's the number-one reason for many athletes' shame and disgrace in the news. This is just what happens when an athlete gets involved with the wrong people or environment.

I am sure that all of the athletes who get caught had good intentions at the start. But there are people who portray themselves as great and trustworthy coaches that study how to manipulate their athletes and get them to use performance-enhancing drugs such as steroids and other illegal substances.

If you have a young athlete that is involved in sports these days, it is imperative to have knowledge of the dangers of performance-enhancing drugs. Too many parents with fallen athletes regret that they didn't educate themselves about performance-enhancing drugs and supplements before it was too late.

It is not an easy task for any parent to inform themselves about all of the drugs that are available which could defraud their athlete's reputation and health, but I'm providing guidance here However, when thinking of the possible outcomes of such activities, you will realize it worth spending time to learn more. Forewarned is forearmed as they say!

I recommend that you take the time to talk to your child about the dangers of performance-enhancing drugs. Alarmingly, Olympic athletes aren't the only ones defrauded by the promise of increased strength and winning performances by using performance-enhancing drugs. Many athletes—in middle school and high school, college, and even "elite athletes"—are using performance enhancing drugs that can harm their reputation and their bodies forever.

Some athletes, especially professionals, risk their careers by taking hormones, potent supplements and synthetic drugs to induce their bodies to build even more muscle to increase their performance. A larger muscle mass allows you to generate more power, which helps you perform short bursts of activity faster. Building muscle mass and reaction speed are important in many sports. In other sports PEds are chosen for different effects, say where a steady hand is important—for example golf and archery.

Performance-enhancing drugs are also used to prevent extreme pain and tiredness and enhance the body's appearance. In spite all of these "great" improvements; performance-enhancing drugs can cause serious harm to the athlete's body and reputation.

Supplements or Drugs?

Food supplements range from daily vitamin tablets which might improve the nervous system and muscle response for athletes, to high protein shakes designed to add muscle bulk—commonly used by weightlifters, for example.

How do you tell the difference between legal and illegal when even over-the-counter cough mixture could get an athlete fined or banned?

Coach knows!

Well, all coaches will know what is and what is not legal, but how can you as a parent know that your young champ is getting the right advice?

'Don't tell anyone, don't talk about it. Trust me.'

Those are the magic words. However the message is dressed up, if your son or daughter has been told that by their coach then you have to suspect it's illegal. Then you need to figure whether you really did find the best coach, and start looking for another.

There is a list of banned substances which sports federations publish, and I'll tell you about the main ones in another chapter. For now, though, make sure your son or daughter (hey, or all of them!) know that if a coach requires secrecy then it's a bad sign and they should tell you right away.

Unscrupulous drugs companies are continuously researching new chemicals which can offer advantages to athletes, and ways in which use of other drugs can be masked. A new compound could be legal this month (because it's not banned in the rules) and illegal next month when it makes the list. All sports federations have codes of ethics for coaches and athletes, but it's tough to know what is right and what is wrong at times like this. A good coach should be able to advise about this. And then, there is the 'spirit of the rules'.

Drugs and their Misuses

Creatine

Creatine is a very popular supplement found in red meat like beef. It can also be found as an over-the-counter supplement that can improve performance. Creatine is a very potent supplement that can provide bursts of high-intensity energy; it is often used by athletes in all sports. Parents should be aware that there are severe side effects that include muscle cramps because of dehydration, severe stomach pains, and overpowering nauseating feelings. The scary part is that a lot of creatine may damage and harm major organs like the heart, liver, lungs and kidney.

Most athletes that are aware of the power of the creatine supplement will discreetly use a tremendous amount per day. Surprisingly, more than 10 percent of young school students had used creatine to enhance their performance.

Anabolic Steroids

Anabolic steroids are an artificial version of testosterone, which is the male gender's hormone. Extra amount of this hormone in the female and male bodies can create enormous strength that can enhance athletic performance. Artificial testosterone can be made in various forms. It can be distributed in gels, injections, patches, creams, drinks, and pills. Some of these have been used by medical doctors to be a replacement therapy for men deficient in testosterone, helping people with AIDS to maintain muscle mass and reduce muscle wasting, and in treating rare types of anemia.

Nevertheless, for a more than a decade, these drugs have become increasingly attractive to athletes. Besides making muscles bigger, anabolic steroids may help athletes recover from a hard workout more quickly by reducing the amount of muscle damage that occurs during the session. In addition, some athletes may like the aggressive feelings they get when they take the drugs.

Anabolic steroids come with serious side effects. Men may develop prominent breasts, baldness, shrunken testicles, infertility and a higher voice. Women may get a deeper voice, increased body hair, enlarged clitoris, increased appetite, and baldness. Both men and women may get severe acne, liver damage, tumors, increased levels of bad cholesterol, and the decrease of good cholesterol, increase of aggressiveness in behavior, drug dependence, and depression. Other side effects can include high blood pressure, fluid retention, small growth in adolescents, cancer, jaundice, and the risk *of contracting HIV or other infectious diseases when syringes are shared between athletes. So as you can see, steroids can do serious harm to the human body. It is just not worth it for any athlete to take the risk of using these drugs.*

Anabolic steroids aren't legal substances, unless your doctor has prescribed them for medical reasons. Taking anabolic steroids to enhance athletic performance, besides being prohibited by most sports organizations, is illegal.

THG

One anabolic steroid receiving a lot of notice today is tetrahydrogestrinone, also referred as THG or 'the Clear'. THG is a marketed dietary supplement for enhancing athletic performance. However, researchers have found that THG is a chemically tainted version of an anabolic steroid that is banned by most sports organizations. In the athletic world, the drug THG is referred to as a "designer" steroid because it is undetectable by traditional steroid-testing techniques. Fortunately a new laboratory test now makes its detection possible. The Food and Drug Administration warns that athletes taking THG are putting their health at jeopardy because THG is an unapproved new drug and little is known about it.

Other common forms of anabolic steroids are:

- *dihydrotestosterone (DHT)*
- *oxymetholone (Anadrol®)*
- *dehydrochlormethyltestosterone (Turinabol®)*
- *oxandrolone (Oxandrin®)*
- *stanozolol (Winstrol®)*
- *metandienone (Dianabol®)*
- *methyltestosterone (Android®)*
- *nandrolone (Durabolin®).*

According to statistics, millions of people use anabolic steroids; most of the users are young people, which means parents should try to be aware of their young athlete's health and take the time to warn their young athletes about the dangerous of cheating with performance-enhancing drugs.

There are several warning signs to help you tell if your young athlete is using performance-enhancing drugs or steroids. One way of noticing is by looking at their bodies and facial areas. If you notice that your athlete has a lot more acne than usual, or is suffering sudden hair loss, then you might have reason to suspect. If your athletic daughter takes these drugs, she will have more testosterone and therefore develop more of a male behavior. She might develop a deepened voice and/or start growing facial hair. You may notice that your young athlete is more irritable than usual or is angry and depressed all the time. You may also notice that your child is no longer growing because anabolic steroids can stop bone growth in adolescents.

Steroid Precursors

Steroid precursors are substances that the body transforms into anabolic steroids. Most athletes who use steroid precursors develop major muscle mass and tremendous strength dramatically. Some athletes use steroid precursors because they think it is not as obvious as using anabolic steroids due to the subtleness of the reaction to the drug, but these substances are just as harmful.

A few of these dangerously common drugs used by young athletes and elite athletes are: DHEA, also known as:

- *dehydroepiandrosterone*
- *androstenediol*
- *androstenedione*
- *norandrostenediol*
- *norandrostenedione*

Please check to see if any of these steroids precursors are subtly included in any supplements that your young athlete is taking.

Ephedra (Ephedrine)

Ephedra is a very popular drug used both by athletes and in other sports for improving performance. Today it is banned because it can cause severe health problems such as irregular heart rhythms leading to heart attacks, seizures, and strokes. Ephedra is a plant that contains the stimulants pseudoephedrine and ephedrine; it is mainly used to reduce physical fatigue during intense workouts and competitions. It also assist weight loss and weight maintenance, and is used to improve mental alertness.

Androstenedione

Androstenedione (andro) is a hormone produced by the adrenal glands, ovaries and testes. It is a precursor hormone that is normally converted to testosterone and estradiol in both men and women.

Manufacturers of synthetic androstenedione, through vigorous marketing efforts, have claimed that their products increase your body's production of testosterone. According to proponents of andro supplements, it allows athletes to train harder and recover more quickly.

Scientific studies that disprove these claims are now emerging. In fact, these studies show that supplemental androstenedione doesn't increase testosterone and that muscles don't get stronger with andro use. The Anabolic Steroid Control Act of 2004 classified andro as a controlled substance, adding it to the list of banned anabolic steroids and making its use as a performance-enhancing drug illegal.

Side effects of andro differ for men and women. In men it can actually decrease the production of testosterone while increasing the production of estrogen. Side effects in men include acne, diminished sperm production, shrinking of the testicles and enlargement of the breasts. In women, side effects include acne and developing male characteristics, such as deepening of the voice and male-pattern baldness. Andro might also stunt a young person's growth. In men and women, supplemental androstenedione can decrease high-density lipoprotein cholesterol known as the "good" cholesterol. Lower lipoprotein levels put a person at greater risk of heart attack and stroke.

Stimulants

Stimulants are drugs that can reduce fatigue, suppress appetite, and increase alertness and aggressiveness. They stimulate the central nervous system, increasing your heart rate, blood pressure, body temperature and metabolism. Stimulants are often used to increase performance in sports.

The most common stimulants include caffeine (as found in coffee) and amphetamines including benzedrine and dexedrine. Cold remedies often contain the stimulant ephedrine. Pseudoephedrine hydrochloride is found in the over-the-counter cold medicine Sudafed®.

Although stimulants can boost physical performance on the field, they have side effects that can harm athletic performance. Although these stimulants enhance an athlete's performance, they also cause heart palpitations and rhythm abnormalities, weight loss, hallucinations, brain haemorrhage, convulsions, mild hypertension, heart attacks, and circulatory problems.

Diuretics

Diuretics are drugs that decrease the body's fluids and salts. This process can cause the body to rapidly dehydrate. This allows an athlete that wants to compete at a lighter weight to lose fluid in order to do so. Diuretics are also used by some athletes to pass drug tests by diluting their urine.

In the medical industry, doctors often use diuretics to treat high blood pressure and conditions that cause fluid retention, such as oedema which can lead to congestive heart failure. When diuretics are taken in small quantities, they have few side effects. However, when taken at higher doses—*favored by some athletes*—the effects may be significantly harmful.

If diuretics are used to achieve weight loss among athletes to promote enhanced performance, this drug may cause muscle cramps, exhaustion, decreases ability to regulate body temperature, potassium deficiency, and heart arrhythmias.

Some of the most widespread diuretics used by athletes are acetazolamide, found in Diamox® and Storzolamide®; benzthiazide, found in Marazide® and Aquastat®; spironolactone, found in Aldactone®; dichlorphenamide, found in Daranide®; and furosemide, found in Lasix® and Fumide®.

Did You Know that . . .

15 million Americans use performance-enhancing drugs.

$1 billion plus—the average amount of money being spent annually in the United States on legally prescribed human growth hormone HGH.

2.4 million—The number of prescriptions for testosterone filled by U.S. pharmacies in 2004

3 million—The number of Americans who use anabolic steroids.

750,000—The estimated number of children who have used steroids and human growth hormone—HGH.

97%—surprisingly, the percentage of teen respondents to a poll conducted by Sports Illustrated who said they would not try steroids or human growth hormone—HGH even if they knew the substances would make them better athletes.

Florida, Illinois, New Jersey, and Texas are the four states that have established steroid screening programs at the high school level; other states, including New Mexico and Indiana, are considering these programs to control steroid use among high school athletes.

Dark Secret

Unscrupulous pharmaceutical companies know the testing strategies of doping agencies like US Anti-Doping Agency.

This is a war of bad scientists against good scientists. Both sides know about the biochemistry, and the body's reactions.

For the bad scientists to create a sought-after performance enhancing drug, they must make sure that the possibility of it being traced or detected is very low. These bad scientists at these unscrupulous pharmaceutical companies find out about the sensitive testing strategies of the doping control agencies and their methods, and so they create new chemicals and masking agents in the drugs to make it harder to trace them.

Why Take the Risk?

Using drugs to enhance the performance and the appearance of the body is becoming more popular among high school, collegiate and professional athletes. It is almost a norm among all athletes and it has become accepted among people who are highly conscious about their body image.

In recent years, studies have shown a rapid increase of reported steroid use among women, especially young female athletes. According to various studies, female athletes are the fastest growing group using performance-enhancing drugs today. More than a third of females who go to the gym at least five days a week have reported past or current steroid use, according to some studies. Performance-enhancing drugs and steroids allow women to rapidly shrink weight and construct a lean and muscular image.

Why do so many young athletes take the risk of using performance-enhancing drugs? Many young athletes who want to be superstars in high school, college and professional sports often pressure themselves to make it big in sports. Often, the athletes who use these drugs will lose their integrity and take the risk in order to win at any cost.

There are a few common reasons why athletes use drugs. Frustration, curiosity, feelings of invincibility, and overpowering peer influence are the primary reasons. And of course, influence by unethical coaches.

Frustration is the number-one reason why athletes take performance-enhancing drugs. Most athletes reach a plateau at some point in their performance and they get frustrated because they feel that they can't get past a certain limit. Performance-enhancing substances may help them move beyond it. It is important to notice these signs. Parents who notice that their teenager is frustrated about his or her sporting performance should take the time to talk with them about it. Talking about how they feel about their practices and competitions will help them understand that with a well-balanced diet, hard work at training, and patience, all things are possible.

Curiosity is another reason why young athletes take performance-enhancing drugs. Athletes have often heard that it is dangerous to take drugs but most are curious to try it anyways. Some of the most successful athletes may become curious and take performance-enhancing drugs just to see what will happen.

'I'm just trying it for a week, ok?'

It is as slippery slope. These curious athletes often believe that they will not get caught, yet they often do. Make sure your young athlete understands that 'curiosity killed the cat', as the saying goes.

Another reason why athletes take performance-enhancing drugs is to have feelings of invincibility. There are psychological effects that these drugs can have on an athlete's mind. Some substances produce feelings of invincibility and excitement, which may be enchanting enough that an athlete doesn't want to discontinue taking banned drugs.

We all know the consequences of overpowering peer pressure on a child's mind. For centuries, athletes have found ways to cheat. Most times they are influenced by other athletes that cheat or coaches that lead them to cheat. The use of performance-enhancing drugs is accepted by a significant number of athletes. If they think members of opposing teams use these substances, insecure athletes may feel that they also need to use performance-enhancing drugs to keep up their competitiveness.

To stay abreast of your teenager's friends and associations, take time to acquaint yourself with people involved in your young athlete's life. The more you get involved with your young athlete's peers, the more easily you will detect if your child might be influenced to use performance-enhancing drugs. Parents may often ignore signs of performance-enhancing drug used by young athletes who appear to be elite-level athletes. So pay attention and get inquisitive!

Dark Secret

The unscrupulous pharmaceutical companies that make banned performance enhancing are actively creating new drugs that are not detected by drug control agencies like USADA: US Anti-Doping Agency.

USADA: US Anti-Doping Agency's goal is to keep all sports clean and free from dirty athletes, but it's a challenge for the agency to control every new drug that is secretly in circulation.

Pharmaceutical companies know what they agency uses to test for traces of drugs in an athlete's system. Over the years, the agency has stepped up their testing strategies by administering blood tests along with the usual urine tests. How do they find out?

Professional athletes have to agree to a testing regime if they want to compete. This includes random unannounced testing visits, but only during certain timeframes—it does not apply 365 days a year—yet.

Advice for Parents with High School and College Athletes

If your young athlete is in high school and is hoping to get an athletic scholarship, he or she is under considerable pressure to succeed. I can remember when I was under pressure to get a scholarship. It was frightening, to say the least. Moreover, not only does the athlete stress because of the pressures of getting into college, they sense the expectations from their parents, coaches, and peers. The pressures of trying to get an athletic scholarship may cause young athletes to consider using performance-enhancing drugs to give them a better chance of getting accepted.

All athletes, including the youngest ones, will tell you that the pressure to win can be very intense. Above and beyond the satisfaction of personal gain, young athletes frequently pursue dreams of making it to the Olympics, obtaining a college scholarship in their sport, or a placing on a professional team. This highly competitive environment in sports, created by our culture, has created a widespread use of steroids and other performance-enhancing agents.

It is important for you and your young athlete to know that collegiate athletes are governed by the National Collegiate Athletic Association, also known as the NCAA. This longstanding association has strict policies to make sure that no athlete has an illegal advantage, in the interests of keeping collegiate sports drug-free.

As a consequence, any student-athletes who get caught on any performance-enhancing drugs will lose a minimum of one year eligibility, according to the NCAA rule book. If your athlete hopes to get a college scholarship, or is already a collegiate athlete, don't get weary of preaching about not using performance-enhancing drugs. It is vital for him or her to fully understand that they are illegal and there would be dire consequences and shattered dreams.

To be sure that your young athlete will refuse to try out performance-enhancing drugs, it is best to be clear about your expectations as parents. Be honest and tell your child that it is unacceptable to use any performance-enhancing drugs and that you expect him or her to avoid them. Make no exceptions. Teach your child that short-term gains with these drugs can lead to long-term problems that will inevitably cause tremendous pain for him or her, and embarrassment to the entire family.

Take the time to discuss the moral values behind the concept of refusing to take these performance-enhancing drugs. Also discuss the proper steps toward athletic preparation. Make this discussion a habit. You can even incorporate it into your regular times of family devotion. Athletes should compete fairly and this is an ethical lesson that is taught by parents first. Strongly emphasize to your child that using performance-enhancing drug is cheating, and that they can also cause serious health problems or even death.

As mentioned in the previous chapters, I cannot stress this enough: take time to talk with your young athlete's coaches. Let the coaches know you've talked with your child and that you don't approve of performance-enhancing drugs. Furthermore, ask your child's coach about the school's position on performance-enhancing drugs. The more you get involved with the coaches about your young athlete and stressing how you disapprove of performance-enhancing drugs, the more it will show how resolute you are about the wellbeing of your child. Moreover, this will deter unscrupulous coaches from providing performance-enhancing drugs to your child.

Another way to make sure that your young athlete is not taking performance-enhancing drugs is to constantly monitor their purchases. You do not have to be overly nosy about everything that they buy; instead take a close look at the items used for their athletic preparations. More importantly, I would recommend that you check to see what the ingredients are in these items. It is also recommended, but probably very difficult to do, that you monitor your young athlete's purchases on the internet. Most steroids and performance-enhancing drugs can be bought over the internet. So pay attention! Be suspicious about cough medicine and decongestant purchases, too!

Dark Secret

Fatal Consequences:

Illegal drug use damages the young body. It also damages the mind, sometimes fatally.

Withdrawal from usage of some drugs such as steroids can lead to emotional disorders and mood changes.

There are several cases where parents have attributed their sports-loving sons' suicides to withdrawal from steroid use.

In most amateur and professional sports, the athletes who win are those with the greatest strength, speed or endurance. Consistently performing with extraordinary strength, speed or endurance is the mark of an elite player. In the later days of my sport career, I became an elite athlete that demonstrated and mastered all these three attributes to becoming an elite player. It took a lot of years and hard work. Athletic performance has more to do with skill and hard work than popping a pill.

There's an overwhelming danger that kids or young adults will think that if they want to be a superstar in sports, they will need to take something artificial and unnatural to reach that level of performance. In our sports world today, there's a tendency to look for an external agent that's going to help to perform better. The reality is that there isn't any.

I was an athlete with an average amount of body fat that was evenly distributed, but I was very strong and speedy. Sheer strength is determined by two factors: amount of muscle and the ability of nerves to stimulate muscle contraction. The most successful elite athletes perform special exercises specific to their sports to improve the neural stimulation of their muscles with complex drills, and many do weight training to build more muscle.

Dark Secret

It's not only drugs.

The scandal over Lance Armstrong, who has had most of his cycling titles removed, has thrown a spotlight on blood doping. An athlete stores blood before an event and then has a transfusion of the fresh blood during a competition. This is of more benefit in endurance events which spread over several days.

Armstrong rode for the US Postal Service Cycling Team, and was transfused with the fresh blood by the Team Doctor. How low can sportspeople—and doctors—go?

The even worse twist was that the vehicle carrying the blood for the team crashed. The result was that some cyclists received other cyclists' blood and became seriously ill. The scandal was uncovered.

This is not an issue for young college sportsmen and women, except that it illustrates how powerful the competitive streak can be and how people can lose sight of right and wrong when faced with the temptation of fame and money.

Part Five

TEACH THEM HOW TO SAY NO!

Facing Reality

'Leave no regrets on the field.'
—*Vince Lombardi*

Though this is only a short section, it is the most important one in the book. It is about that time when your son or daughter has a choice to make. Hopefully, all that we have talked about so far together with your preparations will have made them secure in themselves and able to deal with that moment of choice.

The reality is that many young athletes will at some time be faced with the reality of drugs. You as a parent can prepare them for that moment when someone offers drugs (of any kind).

Yes, it can be hard to say NO! To say **No** *to a trusted leader or friend who has established a great bond is not easy for many young athletes to do. As a result, many at all levels have fallen to the temptation to use performance-enhancing drugs. The moment the athlete shows weakness, the unscrupulous presenter will appear.*

But be sure they will say NO at all costs. Flee and return no more. The persuasion to use drugs will seem like there is no other way—and that your son or daughter must use them to improve their performance and win. Get them to think about all costs of embarrassment and shame of all the other great athletes that got caught even though they were clever to hide their doings. It is not worth it. Gain the fame of crossing the line first, or jumping higher can not outweigh the pain of your name in the newspapers and television headlines screaming the word 'CHEAT!"

For a young sportsperson, saying 'NO' to a respected friend or colleague can seem like an insult is being made. Yet young people have healthy disagreements about many things—about bands and music, ice cream flavors and their favorite movie stars. So why should saying 'NO' to illegal substance use be so difficult? It could be that it is a question of trust, that the friend or coach is trying to be helpful and that help is being rejected.

Many do say NO, but unfortunately they can be tainted by those that say 'YES' and get caught. How can that be? Well, life seems just plain unfair at times and as always a few rotten fruit can spoil the others.

Let's look at baseball. An anonymous testing program in 2003, uncovered 104 players who were taking illegal substances. Another 600 were clear, but because the testing was anonymous every one of them was tainted in the eyes of the public and presumed guilty by many, even though the chances were only 1 in 7 that they were. The public have become conditioned to the idea that drugs are prevalent in professional sport. Thankfully that is not the case, though the danger IS widespread.

How an Athlete Can Say NO!

There are a number of ways, and they are just the same as how to say NO to drugs in the school yard, with a couple of additions. Talk to your budding champion about these ways—this is one important coaching job that a parent can do. You coach them to say NO!

Here are ten examples, using different forms of words.

1. No, thanks. I want to see how far I can get without taking them.
2. No, thanks. I have an allergy to steroids.
3. No thanks. There are major health risks.
4. No, thanks. I've heard some bad stuff about it.
5. No, thanks. I don't need them—my performance is still improving without taking anything.
6. No, thanks. There is too high a risk of getting caught. I don't want to be in the headlines.
7. No, thanks. I don't do illegal.
8. No, thanks. Coach says it's wrong.
9. No, thanks. It's plain wrong.
10. No, thanks, I just don't want to.

Now, the important thing is not to debate the matter, it has to be a firm NO. Saying NO can be difficult, but gets easier with practice.

It is more difficult to say NO to a coach than to a friend or athletic colleague. This is because the coach is being relied on absolutely *for performance advice. Make no mistake, though—a coach who advocates using illegal substances is a criminal, and you should seek another coach immediately.*

Remember, it's better for your son or daughter to lose a friend than a rewarding professional career or even an Olympic Gold Medal.

Fact: *As of May 2011, there had been fifty separate disciplinary actions against USA Track & Field Athletes.*

Dark Secret

Most athletes who get caught blame their coach or manager.

I researched the many athletes and sports personalities who got caught red handed and confessed about their use of performance enhancing drugs. Most said that they were encouraged and given drugs by a trusted coach or manager. Somehow, the people they looked up to were involved.

Their trust was abused and their careers ruined by greedy coaches or managers.

Part Six

'Riches and honor are with me,
enduring riches and righteousness.'
—Proverbs 8:18—in the Holy Bible,
New Kings James Version

This is by far the highest level of sports—the professional level, and the dream of many young sportspeople. This is where the cream of the crop comes together and competes. But from personal experience, this is also the most ruthless level of all.

My advice to young athletes who are seriously thinking about getting into professional sports is to be really sure that it is what they want to do. This is not for everyone in sports and it does not matter how talented an athlete is to succeed. This is where the hearts of athletes are tested.

Finding a Manager

Finding a manager was not hard for me at the start of my professional career thanks to my professional coach. If I didn't have a professional coach with knowledge of who the top managers and sports agents were in the business, I wouldn't have a clue who to pick from. My professional coach referred me to one of the top sports agents out of many who were interest in representing me.

When an athlete is of professional calibre in their sport, sports agents, managers, and scouts will most definitely approach the athlete. This happened a lot months before I went professional. They wanted to support me because these professionals that represent athletes would get percentage of my endorsements and other deals that they help to get for the athlete. It would work just like an actor's acting agent, only without the face shots. Instead, the athletes performance would be the key that sports agent would use.

Another key aspect to look for when trying to select a manager is focus on their reputation. Is it good or bad? Which athletes do they represent now and in the past? I didn't want an agent that represented two or more of my competitors because that would mean that he/she would play the favoritism game. Also, I wouldn't want a manager who represented athletes who had been caught-up in scandals with performance-enhancing drugs.

Simple Finance Issues

Finance issues with a manager are not to be taken for granted. This is one of the main aspects of the relationship and it should be handled with care.

From personal experience, I learned that it was always a good idea to include a lawyer and an accountant with the manager or sports agent. At all costs, it is highly advisable to have a lawyer look over a sports contract with a manager or sports agent before signing the dotted line. It is not that the manager or sports agent is secretly trying to trick or manipulate, but the lawyer can go in more detail and explain the agreements in the contract. A sports person needs to understand the implications of what they are signing, and what the get-outs are if the professional relationship breaks down.

Most sport contracts are for a year. Others can be based on the results of the athlete's competition success. Nevertheless, no matter what the terms and conditions of the contract are, get another professional to look it over.

Changing Coaches

Athletes often change coaches in sports. It is very seldom that athletes stay with the same coach for all levels of their sport career. I did not. I had a different coach at all levels of school; middle school, high school, and college.

An athlete can and should change a coach if the relationship is not working out. I have done this and it worked out well. I changed my professional coaches three times.

The transition was not difficult for me because I was coachable and adapt quickly to the coach's coaching style. Every coach is different and their philosophy varies. I would advise athletes to research a coach's background thoroughly before switching and hiring them to coach you.

I went as far as interviewing the coach on the phone and observing them train other athletes. I also asked a couple well-known people in the industry. At that point I felt that I had enough information to feel comfortable about making the change.

For young amateur sports people, it is easier to change coaches because the contracts are much less formal.

Closing Words

I hope that this book has been of help to you as a parent, and given you an insight into what it will take for your son or daughter to succeed at the top level in sport—and what you as a parent can do to prepare them and help them. You probably realize by now that effective support and guidance from parents can make a huge difference and that will require effort and sacrifice from you.

It is a fact that for every winner there will be several competitors who did not win that particular competition, but there will be other competitions. Even though there may only be one winner, that person cannot win if there are no other competitors. So, taking part is in itself a vital and valuable part of being a sportsperson. Winning a particular race is not the end of the world—there are other competitions, and there are wider sports fields to compete on too.

God has given each of us our gifts in differing degrees and for His own reasons. We each have a personal race in life.

'God wants us to win the race of life.'
—Thomas Nelson, in God's Best
for Your Success

*Appendix

Nutrition Basics

The importance of balanced nutrition cannot be overstated. Growing children have different nutritional needs to that of adults. Nutritional requirements depend also on activity levels.

I've included a short piece here about nutrition. A good coach will be able to provide specific advice, but the worst kind of coach may encourage the use of drugs to accelerate growth. If you give them the best nutritional start, they will reap the benefits for the rest of their lives.

Balanced Nutrition

The main food groups in the human diet are: Fruit and Vegetables; Carbs/Starches—bread, potatoes, rice and pasta; Dairy (and dairy products); Proteins—meat, fish, egg and beans; Fats and Sugars. A balanced intake of all these food groups will provide a healthy nutrition balance, provided that the food is fresh and of good quality.

Fruit and vegetables should make up about a third of daily intake, suitable as part of every meal, as well as for snacks (e.g. a raw carrot, an apple).

Five-a-day is a good rule, and there's nothing like bowl of fresh fruit on the table when the kids get home from school.

Starches should also make up about a third of daily food intake and contain the carbohydrates that are the body's main, most quickly utilized, energy source. Choose unrefined carbohydrates as they will contain the whole of the grain—wholemeal bread for example.

The final third of the ideal meal comprises three groups with foods to be eaten in smaller proportions than the previous two. These food groups contain essentials for a healthy nutritional balance.

Milk and dairy foods are an important source of calcium, essential for healthy bones and teeth.

Meat, fish, eggs and beans includes both animal and plant sources of protein, which provides young bodies with between 10 and 15 per cent of dietary energy requirements. This food group is needed both for growth and repair.

Foods high in fat and/or sugar contain very few nutrients and are sometimes known as 'empty calories'. They should be eaten sparingly because even though they're an important energy source this is junk food territory.

Sugary drinks are also empty calories. However, high energy drinks have a place in competitive sports and will be used under guidance from a coach.

The human body requires water to metabolise food (especially proteins) and is important in maintaining electrolyte balance (helping muscles to work efficiently and avoid cramp). However, excessive water intake can be dangerous, even fatal if the body's electrolytes are diluted too much.

Vitamins & Supplements

Vitamins are complex chemical compounds which we eat in our food, or our bodies make (for example, vitamin D is made in our skin by sunlight). There are 13 vitamins which human beings require. These essential vitamins trigger or assist other chemical processes in our bodies, acting as 'catalysts'.

Supplements are necessary when the body does not get enough of a particular substance through everyday food, or does not efficiently process that food. A healthy body can make vitamins A, D, K, B7 itself, and a balanced diet of good quality fresh food provides adequate supplies of vitamins.

Nine out of the thirteen vitamins are water soluble and are easily passed out by the body. They must be provided on a daily basis—our morning glass of fresh orange juice is part of our daily intake of Vitamin C (don't panic—missing a day or two is nor harmful). The other four of the thirteen vitamins are fat-soluble and can be stored for longer periods of time in the body's fatty tissue and the liver.

If a coach recommends vitamin supplements, then do check that they really are vitamins.

How the Body Uses Food

First, our fuel. The basic fuel for our muscles is glucose. Our bodies convert carbohydrates—starches, from potatoes, pasta, rice, bread—into glycogen and our livers store it. The liver can process fat (and protein) to produce glycogen when the body's energy reserves are depleted. Energy content is measured in calories. Typically, the average laid back adult male in a temperate climate needs about 2,300 calories an day, with a female requiring slightly less than 2,000 calories. This requirement can rise dramatically for sportspeople, even tripling for extreme events.

Next, maintaining our bodies. We need to 'oil our wheels'—replace damaged cells, renew old ones, maintain our immune systems, bone strength, grow hair, maintain brain function and so on. Muscle tone and reaction time is important for most sportspeople, as is the capacity to minimize damage during performance and repair quickly after injury. The human body contains more than 20,000 proteins and the liver and other organs do an amazing job of manufacturing most of those proteins from the basic foods we eat. Certain proteins called amino acids are our 'building blocks'. In combination, these amino acids form the basis of proteins. Of the 22 standard amino acids, 9 are called essential amino acids and must be obtained from our food.

The basic food groups have to contain all the essential ingredients. The fresher the food, the better—many trace elements and minerals decay or react with others as food ages, and the nutritional quality of the food deteriorates. The freshest food is nutritionally richer, by far.

In summary, I hope that gives you a basic understanding of the simple principles of nutrition. For young athletes, these principles apply though the coach will properly recommend dietary changes.

Remember, feed them well and wisely, and teach them how to feed themselves properly. It really is a lifelong and long life investment!

Resources

Coaching Contract Example

This is an example of a coaching contract. Please don't rely on it—I am not a lawyer. It should give you an idea of what you need to see in such a contract.

COACH CONTRACT BETWEEN ATHLETES, PARENTS, AND COACHES

PURPOSE:

This athletic contract is between the ATHLETE, PARENT, and the COACH. It defines certain expectations of the relationship relative to participation in sports and the coach's compensation.

CONDUCT AGREEMENT:

The ATHLETE and the COACH are expected to adhere to all rules and responsibilities. Both are expected to understand that incidents of misconduct may have a definite effect on participation in sports events and practices.

Areas of concern, such as, but not all inclusive are:

   (1) Use of performance enhancing drugs,
   (2) Use of tobacco in any form, alcohol use in any form,
   (3) Use of drugs, depressants, stimulants, or any controlled substance,
   (4) Verbal harassment,
   (5) Sexual harassment and engagement,

Use of any drugs or incidents of behavioral misconduct, will immediately terminate this contractual agreement between all parties.

PROCEDURES TO DISCUSS CONCERNS:

The following is the protocol expected by the ATHLETE, PARENT, and the COACH to abide by:

   (1) The ATHLETE must be free to discuss an issue with the coach. If issue is not resolved, then a parent should get involved.
   (2) A parent may call the coach directly to set up a meeting to discuss and issue concerning the ATHLETE.
   (3) The coach may call the parent directly to set up a meeting to discuss and issue concerning the ATHLETE.

SPORT PARTICIPATION & COMMITMENT

> *(1) If an athlete wants to quit training with the coach, the ATHLETE must notify the COACH in writing.*

COMPENSATION OF THE SPORTS COACH

> *(1) The COACH'S compensation of $_____ is due on the 1ˢᵗ of every month for _____ months.*
>
> *(2) The COACH'S compensation can be paid by the ATHLETE, SPORTS SPONSOR, SPORTS AGENT, or THE PARENT of the ATHLETE.*

CLAUSE TO THE CONTRARY ON NONCOMPENSATION

The COACH shall not receive compensation on the following basis:

> *(1) If the conduct agreement is violated and broken on the premise of providing performance enhancing drugs, tobacco, alcohol, depressants, stimulates controlled substances to the ATHLETE at any time.*
>
> *(2) Involvement of sexual harassment and engagement with the ATHLETE.*

Suziann Reid

Please sign the following and acknowledge that you have agreed to this contract:

_____   _____
             Athlete   *Date*

_____   _____
        Parent/Guardian   *Date*

_____   _____
             Coach   *Date*

Prohibited Substances

The complete up-to-date list of prohibited substances and other useful advice about test protocols can be found at the World Anti-Doping Agency website:
http://www.usada.org/prohibited-list/

Some prohibited substances can be taken by athletes for genuine medical reasons, but they must first obtain a 'TUE'—therapeutic use exemption. This TUE may prevent them from competition temporarily, but it will mean that they do not fail anti doping tests.

I have not included the full list of banned substances here, because it is growing all the time. Athletes should be aware of the latest list. If anyone advises them to take a substance or supplement, they should carefully check it against this list, and if in any doubt, seek qualified advice.

Famous Professional Athletes Caught and Shamed for Using PEDs

1. *Lance Armstrong—Cyclist*
    Admitted using prohibited substances
2. *Marion Jones—Track and Field*
    Admitted using a prohibited substance
3. *Tim Montgomery—Track and Field*
    Admitted using a prohibited substance
4. *Kelly White—Track and Field*
    Admitted using PEDs
5. *Ben Johnson—Track and Field*
    Admitted having used Stanozol
    Olympic Gold Medal rescinded.
6. *Antonio Pettigrew—Track and Field*
    Admitted using a prohibited substance
7. *Tammy Thomas—Cyclist.*
    Used THG.
8. *Alex Rodriguez—Baseball*
    Admitted.   Used   Testosterone   and Primobolan.
9. *Barry Bonds—Baseball—*
    Admitted using PEDs
10. *Tyler Hamilton—Cyclist.*
    Used DHEA
    Stripped of his Olympic Gold Medal
11. *Floyd Landis—Cyclist*
    Used synthetic testosterone

> *Stripped of Tour de France title.*
> 12. *Mark McGwire—Baseball*
> *Admitted use of Androstenedione.*
> 13. *Jason Giambi—Baseball*
> *Used several steroids and HGH.*

Unfortunately this list is only a small sample of reality.

Notable Coaches Who Admitted Giving PEDs to Athletes

1. *Remi Korchemny—Professional Track Coach who coached athletes including Kelly White, Alvin Harrison and Dwain Chambers, all of whom have been disciplined for the use of banned substances.*
2. *Greg Anderson—Personal Trainer. Pleaded guilty to conspiracy to distribute steroids. He was linked via the Balco scandal to Gary Sheffield and Jason Giambi.*
3. *Dr. Jamie Astaphan—The physician who supplied the Canadian sprinter Ben Johnson with banned drugs before he won a gold medal in the 1988 Seoul Olympics.*
4. *Charlie Francis—banned by Athletics Canada following his admissions at the 1989 Dubin inquiry that he had introduced Ben Johnson to steroids.*
5. *Mark Block—Sport Agent and coach. He trafficked drugs supplied by Balco and gave it to his athlete/wife Zhanna Block, sprinter. Accused of various Anti-Doping rule violations and banned for 10 years.*
6. *Raymond Stewart—Jamaican Track Coach banned for life for administering of prohibited substances to athletes.*

Trevor Graham, a Professional Track Coach, did not admit the charge but was banned by

USADA from all its training sites as a number of athletes he was training had tested positive for banned substances. He has a life-time ban for conspiracy and cover-up.

Unfortunately, these lists are only a small sample of reality.

The Balco Scandal

This is not a Dark Secret. It is a shameful episode in US sports history.

Balco—the Bay Area Laboratory Co-operative—was a company which marketed THG, a performance enhancing steroid which was at the time undetectable by drug tests. The company's marketing tentacles reached into the heart of US sports from Track & Field to boxing and baseball. The events subsequently became known as 'The Balco Affair' and implicated many leading sports personalities.

Balco's business was supposedly blood and urine analysis, and testing of food supplements. There was a sideline in performance enhancing drugs.

In 2005, Victor Conte, owner and founder of Balco, pled guilty to illegal steroid distribution and money laundering.

Barry Bonds—a Major League Baseball was implicated in the scandal and later convicted of obstruction of justice for lying to a Grand Jury about his involvement.

Trademark Acknowledgement

These drugs are approved for medical use in many countries, and contribute to healthcare. The mention of the trademarks in this book is in no way suggestive of these trademark owners being involved in any illegal or unethical activity. However, the names have been in common use by illegal users and it is important that parents recognize the names as they are often much easier to remember and pronounce than names such as methandrostenolone (for example). Hence the common usage of some trademarked names. In some cases, the name is no longer registered or has changed ownership.

I have used my best endeavors to track and acknowledge the current trademark owner.

The following trademarks are acknowledged:

Aldactone®	—	*Pfizer Inc.*
Anadrol®	—	*Alaven Pharmaceutical LLC*
Android	—	*ICN Pharmaceuticals Inc.*
		Trademark status is unclear
Aquastat	—	*Unresolved*
Daranide	—	*Unresolved*
Diamox®	—	*American Cyanamid Company*
Dianabol®	—	*Unresolved. Ciba Geigy Corp or Jared R Wheat.*

Durabolin®	—	*Dynamic Sports Nutrition LLC*
Fumide	—	*Unresolved*
Lasix®	—	*Sanofi-Aventis*
Marazide	—	*Unresolved*
Oxandrin®	—	*Savient Pharmaceuticals, Inc.*
Storzolamide®	—	*Stroz Instrument Company*
Sudafed®	—	*McNeil Laboratories*
Turinabol®	—	*Jenapharm/Bayer Schering Pharma AG*
Winstrol®	—	*Sanofi-Synthelabo Inc.*

About the Author

Suziann Marie Reid (first name pronounced "Sooz-ann") was born on January 14, 1977, in Kingston, Jamaica, to Glenroy and Maria Rose Reid.

As a child, Suziann loved running and accompanied her father on his morning runs at the beaches near their home in Jamaica. At first, her father was hesitant to take his eight-year-old daughter with him on long strenuous runs along the sea coast.

Suziann was persistent and determined to get up early and run with her dad—a typical winner's trait. With the help of her dog barking each morning, she always knew when her father was up and ready to jog to the beach.

Realizing how much Suziann loved running, her parents allowed her to participate in sports field day events at Harbour View Primary School to further her training in running.

By age 10, her teachers, coaches, and peers noticed that she had a gift of speed and was growing into a very successful athlete at her school. Suziann could outrun anyone there who tested her ability. As a result, her parents and school encouraged her entry into major national running events in Jamaica.

Jamaica is well-known for developing the most talented sprinters in the world. The country realized that Suziann Reid was definitely one of the best from an early age. Jamaica saw rising superstar and legend in the making for the small, proud country.

In 1989, her family decided to migrate to the United States, leaving behind all of Jamaica's goals and wishes for young Suziann. She was 11 years old when her family moved to Virginia. In Virginia, her mother worked as a nanny for a loving family that helped with the entire family's transition into America. Her father worked more than one job to help maintain the family of five. Eventually, the entire family moved to Maryland.

The flourishing young athlete loved her new life in America, but deep in her heart she still loved running and wanted to start to compete again someday. Two years went by without any competition for until one day her talent was discovered by her principal during a field day at Hyattsville Middle School in Maryland.

Suziann showed up to the field-day in a "skirt." Everyone thought that was strange, but it didn't stop her from winning her race. Realizing that her speed was a true talent, her Principal, Lawrence "Larry" Leahy connected her to Eleanor Roosevelt High School which was the most successful nationally recognized high school for sports.

Eleanor Roosevelt High School was Suziann's starting point of her career in track and field. With the nurturing guidance of Coach Larry Colbert, she won her first race as a freshman at the State Championships and placed fourth at the National Championships. Coach Larry Colbert guided her to 14 State Championship winnings and three National Championship titles.

This was an extraordinary time in Suziann's life as a young athlete. This set the tone for her career in the United States. As a result of her high school successes, she was ranked #1 in the nation in the 400m dash among high school athletes. Hundreds of universities and colleges wanted her to join their athletic teams.

After carefully reviewing all the offers from various universities and colleges, Suziann accepted the University of Texas at Austin. It was another breakthrough for this outstanding athlete. As a freshman, Suziann quickly made another debut by winning the NCAA National Championship in 1996.

This was shocking to many people because it was rare that a freshman could go through the high intensity of the qualifying rounds, make the finals, and then win a national title. Her considerable running talent caught the nation's attention in a great way.

At the same National Championships in her freshman year, after winning a NCAA National title, she led the Texas Longhorns NCAA National Record in the mile relay with a phenomenal performance. The University of Texas won the national team title that year.

Every year, Suziann's performances got better. She won a national title every year and became the first NCAA collegiate woman athlete in history to win an individual national championship title five times and lead the Longhorns to breaking the national record twice in the relays.

To add to her accolades, her college career led her to win "All-American" 17 times. She was also a winner of the "National NCAA Athlete of the Year" and "Big 12 Conference Athlete of the Year" awards, which are the most prestigious recognitions of collegiate athletes.

In addition, Suziann was awarded the "Honda Award" in 1999, which recognizes the top collegiate athlete in each individual sport. She was inducted into the admirable "Hall of Honors" in 2008 at the University of Texas.

At the end of Suziann's college athletic career, she went on to complete her Bachelor's of Science Degree at the University of Texas. After college, she was offered many endorsements and contracts from various sportswear makers all over the world.

At the age of 22, Suziann became a professional athlete representing Adidas and, eventually with Nike. This was pivotal point in her career competing as a professional in her sport. With courage and grace, Suziann continued a dynamic career that led her to several winning World Games representing the United States. Her career took her all over the world competing against the best from every country.

During her professional career, Suziann won gold and silver medals with other legendary athletes. Today, several of her records still stand.

Suziann retired from her professional career in August 2005 after the World Championship in Helsinki, Finland.

After retiring, she turned to business and earned a Masters of Business Administration from Regis University in 2010.

Author's website: www.SuziannReid.com